*A Short History of
Tompkins County*

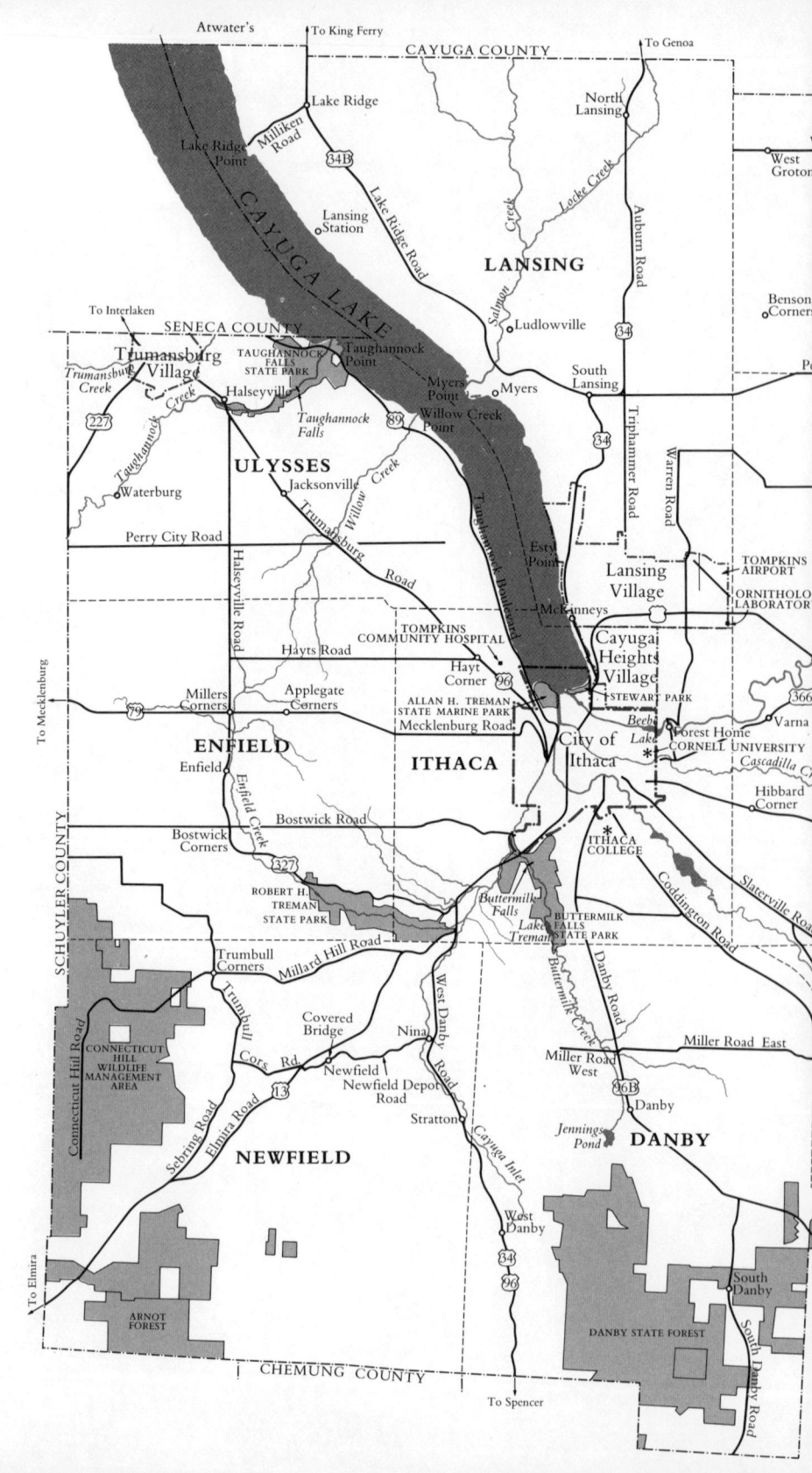

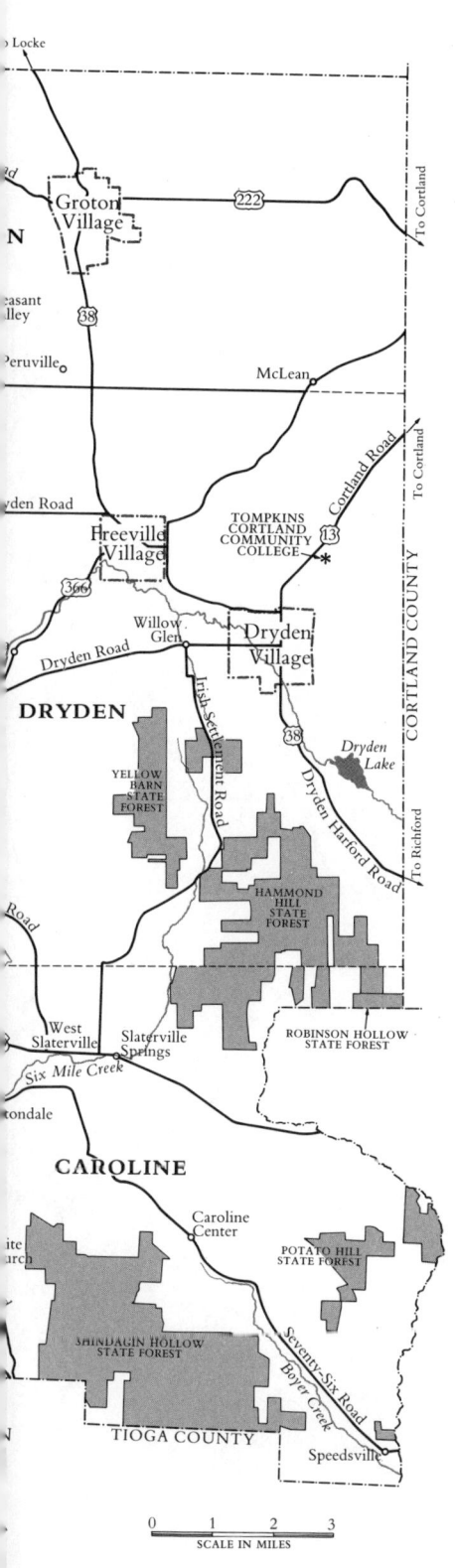

Tompkins County Today

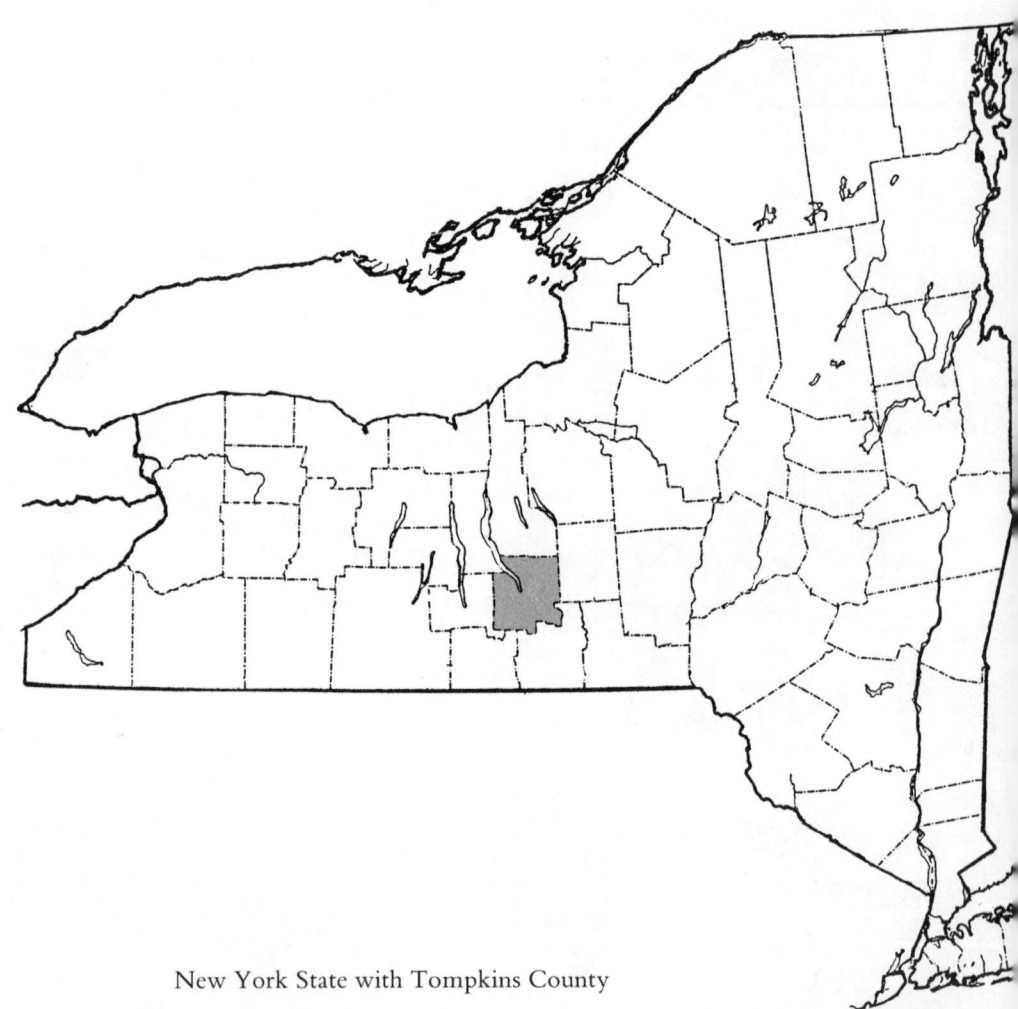

New York State with Tompkins County

A Short History of Tompkins County

Jane Marsh Dieckmann

DeWitt Historical Society
of Tompkins County

ITHACA, NEW YORK

This publication was made possible through a gift from the Tompkins County Trust Company, as part of its sesquicentennial celebration.

Copyright © 1986 by DeWitt Historical Society of Tompkins County

All rights reserved. Except for brief quotations in a review, this book, or parts thereof, must not be reproduced in any form without permission in writing from the publisher.

Library of Congress Cataloging-in-Publication Data

Dieckmann, Jane M.
A short history of Tompkins County.

Bibliography: p.
Includes index.
1. Tompkins County (N.Y.)—History. I. Dewitt Historical Society of Tompkins County. II. Title.
F127.T7D54 1986   974.7'71   85-25440
ISBN 0-942690-34-6 (alk. paper)
ISBN 0-942690-33-8 (pbk.: alk. paper)

Printed in the United States of America

Unless otherwise indicated, the illustrations have been provided by the DeWitt Historical Society.

*This book is dedicated to three women,
who are MY history—my mother,
Mary Hunter Marsh, and my
two daughters, Katherine
and Judith Dieckmann.*

Contents

Foreword   11

Chronology   14

1. *Beginnings and the Early Years*   21
   The setting. Indian settlers. The first pioneers. The early communities. Travel. The establishment of Tompkins County.

2. *Growth and Development: The Communities*   38
   The city and town of Ithaca. Caroline. Danby. Dryden. Enfield. Groton. Lansing. Newfield. Ulysses.

3. *Transportation and Communication*   87
   Roads, streets, bridges. Canals. Railroads. Public transportation. Air travel. Postal service, telegraph, telephone.

4. *Institutions, Organizations, Agencies*   111
   Education: Cornell University. Ithaca College. Tompkins Cortland Community College. Private schools. George Junior Republic. Public schools.
   Libraries.
   Community Services and Benevolent Societies: Social services. Medicine and health. Private groups.
   Churches and Religious Organizations.

Contents

5. *Recreation and Cultural Activities*   156
   Parks and Forests: Municipal parks. State parks.
   Pastimes and Events: Boat and train excursions. Fairs and festivals. Sports.
   Organizations in Recreation and the Arts: Theaters. Musical groups. Museums and historical societies.

6. *Business, Commerce, Industry*   186
   Early Development: The mills and the boats. Merchants.
   The Perennials: Agriculture. Salt. Tourism. The *Ithaca Journal*. Corner Book Store.
   Unusual Enterprises: Groton. Ithaca.
   Large and Small Successes: Morse Chain, NCR, Ithaca Gun.
   Professions.

Afterword: Past to Present   213

Notes   217

Bibliography   219

Index   221

Foreword

A bumper sticker—surely a sign of our times—has been around for a while now. In white letters on a fresh, rich, dark green ground, it says Ithaca is GORGES. It could just as well say Tompkins County is GORGES, for this brief statement, though too long for a bumper sticker, gives us a succinct description of our surroundings, the place where we live, a locality we all love for its breathtaking natural beauty complete with the lake and the rugged rock walls of the gorges. For the first—and perhaps the most important—statement we can make about Tompkins County is that is beautiful, and this beauty, although we may not at all times pay attention to it, is always a part of our daily lives.

The telling of history means telling about change, but always against a background of constants. People and natural events have changed the face of the landscape, of course, but the structure of our natural surroundings has remained the same. We have the lake, the streams, the plains, the hills, and the gorges, and they shape our lives every day—especially the gorges, because the need to get across these cuts, some of them very deep, in the land's surface helps decide how we travel the county. Another constant is the weather, and we see, through the years, various adaptations—some simply practical, some amusing, some even desperate—to this fixed element of the environment. Although the county's land has never been touched by war (except at the very beginnings of our written history when bands of soldiers came through and destroyed the Indian settlements), it has been changed—and fairly

Foreword

often—by floods, and by fires, and these events have had their effect upon our communities and people.

Tompkins County resembles any number of counties in the eastern United States: one small city and a number of villages and towns, a rural setting with agricultural occupations, a certain isolation from large industrial areas. But for those of us who live here and have come to terms with our surroundings, Tompkins County has unique characteristics and qualities. We all sense that this is a special place; over 180 years ago Simeon DeWitt sensed it when he planned the settlement at the head of Cayuga Lake and, it is believed, named it Ithaca for another special place, home to the Greek hero Odysseus. Ever since the beginning people have come here, for any number of different reasons, and have been drawn to stay. Tompkins County has an unusual number of artists and writers, scientists and scholars, professionals and farmers, who have found in the area an inspiration, a source of joy and meaning. It is hard to pin down the uniqueness of the region; most of the individuals who live here do not attempt to analyze the unusual combination of qualities which makes our community so special.

Through the years the history of the county has been made by men and women of extraordinary vision and determination, men and women who have seen beyond the ordinary and have brought their ideas to life. Beneath the changes they have made, however, are qualities that endure: a sense of flexibility and adaptability to the surroundings, the courage to change and the will to persevere, the vision to create something original and significant. When one reads about the county's early communities, one is struck by the diversity and versatility of the population. Today we hear often about the house painter with a Ph.D. in history, the plumber with a degree in business management, the farmer who specializes in languages and literatures—we all smile and think we've hit on something new and different, but in reality this "unusual" combining of occupations and pursuits has long been characteristic of our populace. There was the tanner who became Ithaca's first president. There was the engineer who came to work on Ithaca's trolley system and went on to plan Stewart Park; he ended up as Ithaca's first paid mayor. And, of course, there was the farm boy and inventor who founded a great American university. Is it something

Foreword

in the air? We may not know what it is, but we do know there is something here.

Preparing this book has been a fascinating and rewarding task. Such research has its problems, however, because frequently information is conflicting, documentation is inadequate, and verification difficult. It is my hope that mistakes and misconceptions have been kept to a minimum.

Many people have helped me with this project. I have profited very much from conversations with local historians, and I am indebted to them for their generosity to me and their invaluable help. And for their assistance and support, I should like to thank Raymond Van Houtte of the Tompkins County Trust Company, Maralyn Fleming and the members of the trust company's special sesquicentennial committee, Charles Barber, Ronald Clayton, Jane Hardy, Nancy and Joseph Leeming, Nancy McGinnies, Henry Neubert, Lois O'Connor, and Daniel Snodderly. And I am especially grateful to Roger Haydon, who edited the manuscript, as well as to Richard Rosenbaum, who designed and produced the book, and —most of all—to Margaret Hobbie and her staff at the DeWitt Historical Society.

JANE MARSH DIECKMANN

Ithaca, New York
April 1985

Chronology

1615   Frenchman Etienne Brule is the first white man to penetrate the Finger Lakes region.

1743   Five explorers cross Tompkins County. Between 1745 and 1766 four groups of Moravian Church missionaries move through the area.

1779   Major General John Sullivan sends two troop contingents through the county, who destroy Indian settlements.

1784   Simeon DeWitt is named surveyor general of New York State.

1788   First white settlers come to Tompkins County and build cabins on site of present DeWitt Park in Ithaca. In the next two years pioneers establish settlements throughout the county.

         New York ratifies the U.S. Constitution on July 26 and recommends the addition of a bill of rights.

1789   George Washington is inaugurated as first President of the U.S. on April 30 in New York City.

         Cayuga Indians surrender their lands to the state.

1791   The first road is built in the county.

1803   The town of Dryden is formed from Ulysses.

1804   A charter is granted for the Catskill Turnpike.

         The first postmaster in Ithaca is appointed by President Thomas Jefferson.

1805   Simeon DeWitt's map of New York State is published.

1807   U.S. Congress passes legislation prohibiting the importation of slaves after January 1, 1808.

1809   The first Ithaca Hotel is built on the southeast corner of Owego (later State) and Aurora streets.

1811   The towns of Caroline and Danby are organized as part of Tioga County and annexed to Tompkins County in 1822.

         The Ithaca & Owego and Ithaca & Geneva turnpikes are completed.

Chronology

1812/5	The United States is at war with England.
1812	A law establishes a public school system in New York State.
1815	The *Ithaca Journal* publishes its first issue as an untitled single sheet.
1817	Tompkins County is created by an act of the state legislature on April 17. Under this act the towns of Division (renamed Groton in 1818) and Lansing are formed from the townships of Locke and Milton respectively.
1818	Tompkins County Medical Society is incorporated; it reorganizes in 1862.
1820	The steamboat *Enterprise* makes its first trip on Cayuga Lake.
1821	Ithaca is incorporated as a village on April 2.
	The town of Enfield is created from Ulysses.
1822	The towns of Caroline, Danby, and Cayuta (later Newfield) are annexed to Tompkins County.
1825	The Erie Canal opens along its entire length of 363 miles, linking New York City with the Great Lakes; a connection to Cayuga Lake is made in 1828.
1827	Slavery is abolished in New York State.
	The Eight-Square Schoolhouse is built in Dryden.
1828	Ezra Cornell, aged twenty-one, arrives in Ithaca in search of work.
	Ithaca & Owego Railroad receives a charter, the second in the state.
1830	The Clinton House opens its doors.
	The Central Exchange Hotel in Libertyville is begun. It is soon renamed Rogues Harbor Inn.
	Newfield Flouring Mills start operation.
1831	Ithaca sets up its first Board of Health.
1834	Simeon DeWitt dies in the Clinton House.
	The I&O Railroad opens officially, the fourth railroad in operation in the state.
1836	St. James AME Zion Church is constructed and for more than twenty years serves as an important station on the Underground Railroad.
1837	A nationwide financial panic grips the county, bringing widespread unemployment and dashing many commercial hopes.
1842	The *American Agriculturalist*, a farm paper for the northeastern U.S., is founded in Ithaca.
1843	The Village (later City) Hall is erected in Ithaca; the building is razed in 1965.
1846	A telegraph service is installed in Ithaca.
1848	The Hermon Camp mansion is completed in Trumansburg.
1850	Fugitive Slave Law is passed by the U.S. Congress.
1851/3	The Newfield Covered Bridge is constructed.

Chronology

1853	A part of the town of Newfield is annexed to Chemung County.
1854	Old Tompkins County Courthouse is erected and is used until 1932 as a courthouse.
	The town of Hector is moved to Schuyler County.
1857	Dryden is incorporated as a village and is reincorporated in 1865.
1861	Abraham Lincoln is inaugurated as the nation's sixteenth President. The Civil War begins with the firing on Fort Sumter on April 12.
1862	Dryden Springs Place opens under the direction of Dr. Samantha Nivison.
	The Morrill Land Grant Act, giving land to states for the establishment of agricultural colleges, is passed by the U.S. Congress.
1863	The Emancipation Proclamation takes effect on January 1. In 1868 the Fourteenth Amendment, granting full citizenship to blacks and all others born in the U.S. or naturalized (excepting Indians) is ratified.
	The first county historical society is founded.
	The Cornell Public Library is begun and will be dedicated in December 1866.
1864	The Boardman House is built.
1865	The Civil War ends on April 8 with Lee's surrender at Appomattox. One week later Lincoln is assassinated.
1866	Cascadilla Hall is completed; it serves as Cornell's earliest building.
	Ithaca Calendar Clock Company starts operation.
1867	Cayuga Lake Railroad is chartered.
	The Grange movement (with more than 858,000 enrolled members today) begins in Fredonia, N.Y.
1868	The Ithaca YMCA holds its first meeting.
	The Wilgus Block with the Wilgus Opera House is built in downtown Ithaca.
	Cornell University opens and is officially inaugurated on October 7.
1870	The pleasure boat *Frontenac* makes its maiden voyage on Cayuga Lake.
1871	Ithaca & Athens Railroad begins business. The Utica, Ithaca & Elmira starts service through the county.
	A major fire destroys seven buildings (including the Ithaca Hotel) in Ithaca's commercial district.
1872	Trumansburg is incorporated as a village.
1873	A national financial panic bankrupts many investors, including Ezra Cornell, and is followed by a five-year depression.
1874	The Public School Act establishes a system of graded public schools through New York State.
	Ezra Cornell dies.

Chronology

1875   A major fire burns the center of Newfield, destroying all its records.
Sage College for women is opened at Cornell University.

1876   The Groton Carriage Company is incorporated.
Ithaca is one of the first communities in the country to get telephone service.

1877   The Groton Bridge & Manufacturing Company begins to manufacture iron bridges.

1880   Ithaca Gun Company is established near Fall Creek.

1887   Freeville is incorporated as a village.

1888   Ithaca is chartered as a city and celebrates on June 1.

1890   Ithaca holds its first Labor Day parade. In 1894 Congress will declare the first Monday in September a national Labor Day and a legal holiday.
The Lehigh Valley Railroad takes over several smaller railroads in the county.

1892   Ithaca Conservatory of Music is founded.

1893   Lyceum Theater opens on South Cayuga Street in Ithaca and for thirty years is a cultural center for the county.
The first trolley car makes a run up East Hill. The streetcar loop will be completed in 1900.

1894   The College of Veterinary Medicine is established at Cornell.

1895   George Junior Republic is founded in Freeville.
Newfield is incorporated as a village; the charter is dissolved in 1925.

1898   Morse Chain Company is incorporated.

1902   Rural Free Delivery of mail is inaugurated in Tompkins County.

1903   A typhoid fever epidemic engulfs Ithaca and its surroundings.

1904   New York is the first state to pass a law on speed limits for automobiles: 10 mph in cities, 15 mph in small towns, 20 mph in the country.

1905   A major flood washes out many bridges and leaves large areas of the county under water.

1907   The *Frontenac* burns at Long Point on Cayuga Lake.

1909   The Short Line of the New York, Auburn & Lansing Railroad inaugurates service.
Grace Miller White's novel, *Tess of the Storm Country*, depicting life in the Silent City, is published.

1912   Ithaca Municipal Airport opens near Inlet.

1914   World War I begins; the U.S. declares war on Germany in April 1917. The armistice is signed November 14, 1918, but the U.S. never signs the peace treaty.

1915   Cayuga Heights is incorporated as a village.

1920   The Eighteenth Amendment to the Constitution, allowing Prohibition, is ratified in January. Repeal comes in 1933.

Chronology

1920   Suffrage for women is granted by the Nineteenth Amendment. The League of Women Voters is organized.
Enfield Glen (later Robert H. Treman State Park) is opened as a public recreational area.

1921   Four Ithaca women's organizations fund and open the Women's Community Building.
Renwick Park is renamed Stewart Park, which is renovated and developed as one of the county's major recreational areas.

1924   Buttermilk Falls State Park and the first portion of Taughannock Park are opened to the public.

1925   The College of Home Economics at Cornell is founded; it is renamed the College of Human Ecology in 1969.

1929   Stock market crash on October 29 is the forerunner of the Great Depression.

1931   Ithaca College is established from the Ithaca Conservatory of Music.

1932   The Tompkins County Courthouse is built on the southwest corner of Court and Tioga streets.

1933   Much of Roosevelt's New Deal legislation is passed, including the Civilian Conservation Corps. In 1935 the Works Progress Administration begins.

1935   Hermann Biggs F. Memorial Hospital opens as a county tuberculosis facility; it becomes the Tompkins County Hospital in 1948.
A major flood in the first days of July, with lives lost, devastates the county with enormous damage along all the creeks and wipes out the center of Trumansburg.

1939   World War II begins in Europe, to end in 1945. The U.S. enters the war in December 1941. Many local businesses adapt to wartime production.

1945   The first atomic bomb is detonated in New Mexico. Several members of Cornell's Physics department are contributors to the project, developed at Los Alamos.

1947   Tompkins County inaugurates its Department of Health.
Robinson Airlines starts operations in Ithaca (later becoming Mohawk Airlines, and, ultimately, part of US Air).

1958   The L.C. Smith Company, Rose Typewriter Company, and W. Marchant Calculators merge to form the SCM Corporation.

1959   Ithaca College starts building a new campus on South Hill.
The Black Diamond makes its last trip on the Lehigh Valley Railroad.

1966   Historic Ithaca is founded.

1967   Cornell professor Hans Bethe receives the Nobel Prize in Physics. Later Cornell laureates are Roald Hoffmann in Chemistry (1981) and Kenneth Wilson in Physics (1982).

Chronology

1968 Tompkins County Public Library is constructed in Ithaca to replace the Cornell Public Library, razed in 1960.
TC3 opens in Groton and moves to its Dryden facility for the 1974 summer session.
1969 Campus unrest at Cornell draws national attention.
1971/2 Cass Park is developed along with the municipal marina, which becomes the Allan H. Treman State Marine Park.
1974 Ithaca Commons, the first such pedestrian mall in the state, is constructed and opened to the public.
Lansing is incorporated as a village.
1980 The Tompkins County Hospital opens its new building on the Trumansburg Road; it becomes the privately owned and operated Tompkins Community Hospital in 1981.

[1]

Beginnings and the Early Years

As we look today over Tompkins County—our city and towns with their houses, public buildings, church spires, and commercial centers, as well as our lake dotted with sailboats in the summer and our streams with their modern bridges—it is very difficult to imagine our region at the time of the county's settlement at the end of the eighteenth century. Surely the vast areas of forests and swamps, the tiny settlements scattered here and there along the creeks, and the lakeshore virtually empty of any sign of human life make up a scene very different from the one we see now.

The shape of our region—its lake, gorges, rolling hills, and flatlands—is a development that has taken millions and millions of years. This development involved the eruption of volcanoes, the invasion of oceans, the formation of rock layers out of huge amounts of sediment, and the shaping of streams and the lake by the movement of water. The area was first a huge shallow sea, and then gentle rolling hills in which the Finger Lakes were valleys with major streams flowing north. During the Ice Age, about one and one-half million years ago, a glacier moved south, digging the valleys deeper and forming what would become the Finger Lakes. The glacier melted and later was followed by a second one, which deepened these areas even more. The valley of Cayuga Lake and the surrounding hills were a result of this glacial movement and subsequent erosion by water. The descent from the heights above the deep lake valley down to the water level is steep, from 700 to 900 feet, and 400 to 600 feet of the drop are within the last mile.

For the Indian dwellers, the early explorers, and the first pioneers who came into this valley, the sight of this unusual landscape—the lake with its wild shores and the streams rushing through the layered rock walls of the gorges—must have been striking. Heavy forests blanketed the hills and plains, while much of the flatland at the head of the lake was a swamp, with dense growths of trees and vines, some scrubby bushes, and large areas of marsh grass. To the south and east, where the water was carried off by Six Mile and Cascadilla creeks, was drier ground.

The waterways, an essential and basically unchanged element of the landscape, were of prime importance in the early days. Six principal streams come together at the head of Cayuga Lake; they are Fall, Cascadilla, Six Mile, Buttermilk, Inlet, and Enfield (or Five Mile) creeks. The two other major creeks of our region empty into the lake close to the northern borders of the county, Salmon Creek on the east shore, Taughannock Creek on the west. Most of these streams move through steep gorges (figure 1) before running their final and usually gentle course to the lake, and waterfalls and cascades are a basic part of the scene. Appreciated today principally for their recreational and scenic merits, the creeks were vital to the early settlers, mainly as a necessary source of water and waterpower.

Nor were the various waterways the only advantage that the region had to offer. In the northern portion of the county were areas of extremely rich and fertile soil, easily adapted to farming; there were deposits of salt under the lake and great amounts of timber and good building stone could be found throughout the region. With this setting and these resources, it really is no wonder that the place we call Tompkins County today appealed to those who first saw it and chose to remain.

It was probably back in the twelfth and thirteenth centuries that the first Indians settled in upstate New York. In about 1600 five Iroquois nations—the Mohawk, Oneida, Onondaga, Cayuga, and Seneca—formed a confederacy, known as the Iroquois Confederacy of Five Nations and later, when joined in the eighteenth century by the Tuscaroras, as the League of Six Nations. It was the

1. Cascades in Enfield Glen Now part of the Robert H. Treman State Park, this glen, with its layered rock walls, is one of many beautiful gorges in the region. Others can be seen in figures 40, 67, 70, 71, and 91.

Cayugas, who lived in various settlements in our region, and Cayuga Lake bears their name. But the Indians were not the only people to have known the area; as early as 1615, it is believed, a young Frenchman named Etienne Brule, the first white man known to have penetrated the region, arrived on a war mission for Samuel Champlain, the French explorer and colonizer of Canada. And in July 1743 an important party of five men—colonial agent and Indian interpreter Conrad Weisner, early naturalist and botanist John Bartram, surveyor and map maker Lewis Evans, Oneida chief Shikellamy, and his eldest son Spreading Oak—crossed the county. Moravian Church missionaries made four journeys as well between 1745 and 1766. During one such trip (in 1750) missionary John Frederick Cammerhof recorded the following description of the valley of Ithaca and the lake: "All these creeks flow into one lake. We saw the last creek after rushing on wildly, fall perpendicularly from a height of ninety feet. It was indeed an interesting and thrilling sight." The water of the lake "is as clear as crystal, and the Indians say deeper than they can tell. . . . Hills and mountains bound the lake on both sides. Many large and small creeks rush down from them and empty into the lake. . . ."[1]

The British traded with the Indians during the eighteenth century, and most of the Iroquois Confederacy sided with the British during the American Revolutionary War. The Indians assisted their allies in raids against many American frontier settlements, attacks intended to weaken the American forces, destroy supplies, and divide the manpower of the colonists.

In 1779 Major General John Sullivan, in a strategy designed to break the power of the Iroquois, was sent by George Washington to suppress the Indians. In his infamous campaign of devastation, he moved his troops from the Susquehanna River in Pennsylvania through the Finger Lakes region as far north as the Genesee Valley. Sullivan, who had camped at Geneva, then dispatched two bodies of soldiers to invade the Cayuga's territory, with instructions to destroy settlements and crops, round up any tribesmen that could be found, and drive the Indians out. One contingent of troops under Lt. Colonel Henry Dearborn was sent down the west side of the lake; they destroyed several settlements, including a large village called Coreorgonel in the Inlet Valley, opposite Buttermilk

Falls. Coreorgonel is an Indian word meaning "where we keep the pipe of peace," and the village had twenty-five long houses of bark, set in a semicircle inside a stockade. The soldiers then came in on the Spencer Road trail, camped on Prospect Hill (Terrace Hill today) to watch for the other group, and the next day moved on west to Seneca Lake. The other contingent, under Colonel William Butler, swept down the east side, camped near Ludlowville, and reached Ithaca the next day. After crossing Fall Creek near the current Lake Street bridge, they followed a well-traveled Indian trail up Linn Street, across Ithaca's present business district, and out the Spencer Road trail to the burned ruins of Coreorgonel. A soldier in the group named Thomas Grant wrote the following description of the Indian settlement in his diary: "The town was situated on a rising ground in a large beautiful valley. The soil is equal to, or rather superior to any in the country."[2]

After camping overnight, Butler's troops continued up Newfield Hill and through Poney Hollow to join the main army near Horseheads. The two groups, which were supposed to join forces, missed each other by a day. But their mission was successful; most of the Indians were driven out. Of those who remained, most in general were helpful to the white settlers as guides and provided information, supplies of food and seed, and that very important commodity—salt. Their trails, used by the settlers, would later be developed as roads and highways. During the years after the war the once-powerful Indian tribes gave up their territory, piece by piece; in 1789 the Cayuga Indians surrendered their land to the state.

During the Revolutionary War men were encouraged to sign up to fight for what was to become the new nation by the promise of land out on the frontier. After the termination of the war, a portion of the former Iroquois lands east of Seneca Lake (which amounted to over one and one-half million acres) was designated by an act of the state legislature as the Military Tract (Map 1). It was divided into twenty-eight townships, six miles square, most of which were given classical names. Township #22, encompassing the northwestern part of our region and the Ithaca area, was given the name of Ulysses; the townships of Hector (#21) and Dryden (#23) as well as parts of Milton (#17) and Locke (#18)

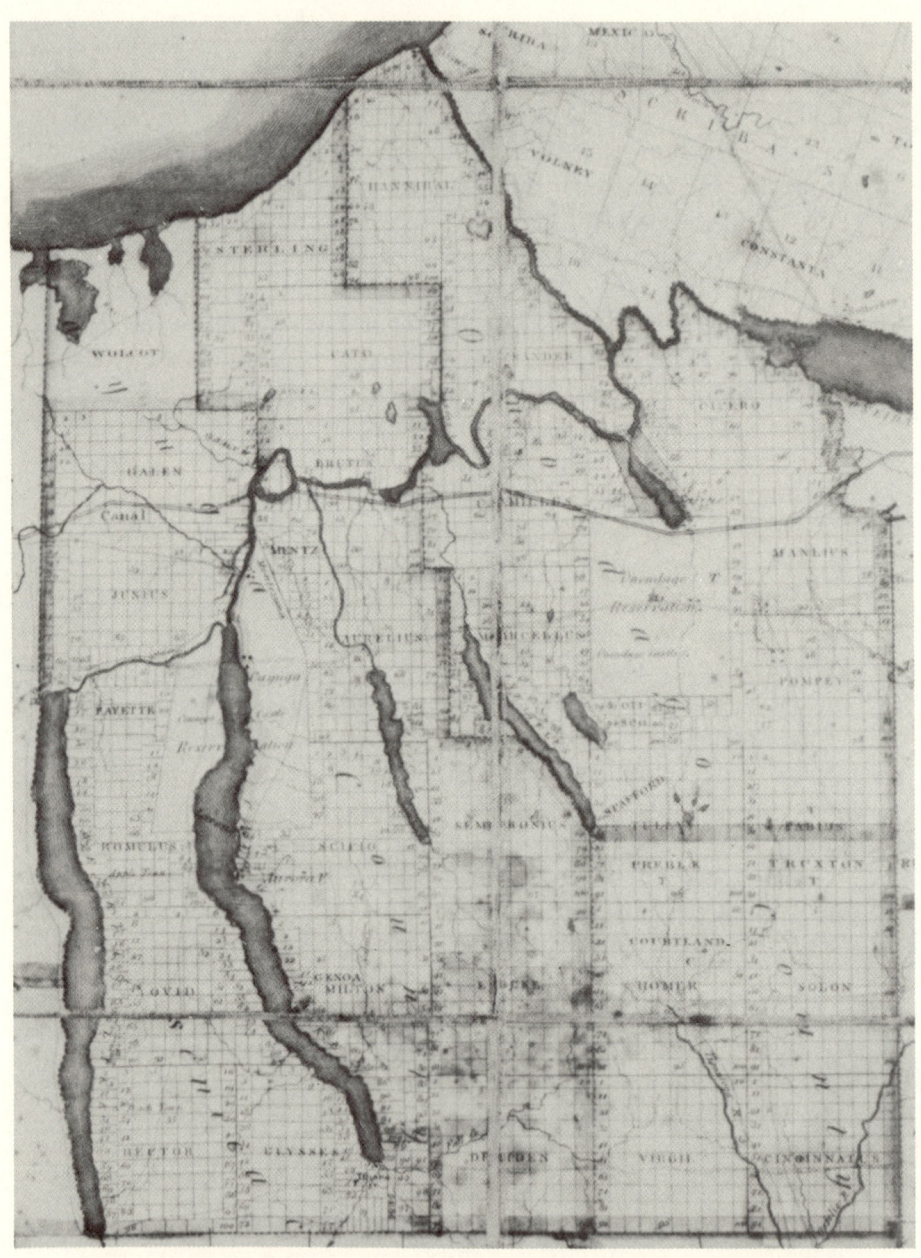

Map 1. The Military Tract. Shown here is the central section of a map of New York State published in 1812. The division of the various townships into lots can be seen. A soldier could receive a rather large piece of property. In the upper left corner is Sodus Bay.

Beginnings and the Early Years

would also become part of Tompkins County. Soldiers were to draw lots for their land. Privates were allowed lots of six hundred acres, their officers having the opportunity to get more. Even before the lots were drawn, however, the first pioneers had made their way into our area and had started the first settlements.

According to the historical marker in DeWitt Park, the "original white settlers" of the region were Jonathan Woodworth, a surveyor, and Robert McDowell, a Revolutionary War officer, who came in 1788. It is believed they built cabins in the area near the marker. Later in the year McDowell brought his entire family here, and they settled a tract of 1,400 acres in an area lying west of Tioga Street. And in April of 1788, according to the older histories, a group of eleven men left Kingston (on the Hudson) with two Delaware Indian guides to explore the country west of the Susquehanna. Among them were Jacob Yaple, Peter Hinepaugh, and Isaac Dumond, who after seeing the region returned home. They came back the following April with Jacob's younger brother John, planted corn, and left John behind to mind the crops. They returned once more to Kingston, packed up their belongings and families, and in August arrived at the head of Cayuga Lake. There were nineteen people in the group; they had gotten to Owego after a month of travel that combined overland and river routes (by canoe) on both the Delaware and Susquehanna rivers. It had taken them nineteen days to open, widen, and travel the Indian path from Owego, a distance of twenty-nine miles. Peter Hinepaugh erected a log cabin close to the head of Linn Street near the location today of the Christian Science church; Jacob Yaple and Isaac Dumond built cabins at the foot of the State Street hill, near the present Tuning Fork. The settlers built on land that had been cleared by the Indians, but began almost immediately to prepare more land for planting and building. It was not long before Jacob Yaple erected the first waterpower mill on Cascadilla Creek above Hinepaugh's cabin, a mill that was soon grinding 20 to 25 bushels of wheat a day.

In the meantime lots were being drawn for the land of the Military Tract. Some veterans came to settle, but the great majority sold their claims (some sold them several times over), often to speculators. As a result, numerous problems arose over defective

2. Simeon DeWitt (1756–1834). This print was made from a portrait painted by Ezra Ames in 1826.

titles, and several original settlers were forced to leave their cabins and move elsewhere. Both the Yaples and the Dumonds, for example, because their agent had failed to register their claim in Albany, found they did not have title to the land they had built on. They moved on in 1795 to start another settlement, this time in Danby.

At this point in our story there enters a very important figure in the history of Tompkins County (figure 2). Simeon DeWitt (1756-1834) was instrumental in the establishment of Ithaca and more responsible than anyone else, not only for its existence and probably its name, but also the shape it took, a shape it retains to-

Beginnings and the Early Years

3. Abram Markle House. Ithaca's first frame house stood at 114 Linn Street and is shown here in 1957; it has since been demolished.

day. Simeon DeWitt had been named surveyor general of New York State in 1784, an office he held for fifty years until his death. He had been assigned the job of surveying the 1,680,000 acres of Iroquois lands in the central part of the state, and in 1796 he set up a field office on what is now DeWitt Place in Ithaca. He prepared a complete map of the state, dated 1802, and when it was published in 1805, the name of Ithaca appeared on it. Indeed, DeWitt even planned to make Ithaca his own home, but his duties kept him busy elsewhere. He did take over the Abram Markle house near Linn Street (Ithaca's earliest frame dwelling and built around 1800, figure 3) and made it his farmhouse when its builder failed financially.

In 1789 Abraham Bloodgood of Albany got a patent to 1,400 acres of land here, including all Ithaca's present downtown area west of Tioga Street; his son Francis was to manage it, but Francis got into financial difficulties and so Bloodgood asked Simeon De-

[29]

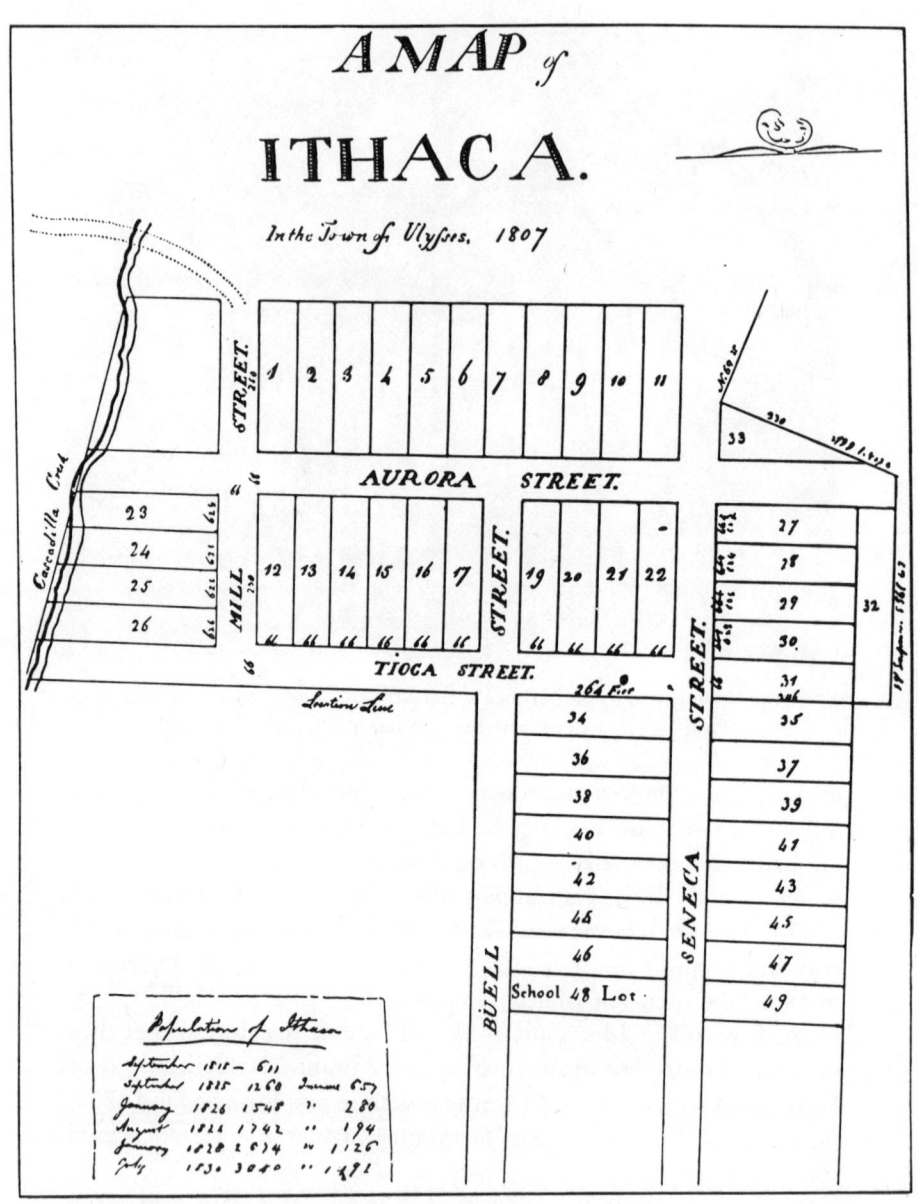

Map 2. Simeon De Witt's Map of Ithaca (1807)

Beginnings and the Early Years

Witt (whose first wife was Bloodgood's stepdaughter) to help out. In exchange for this help, DeWitt acquired 1,000 acres of that patent. He then went on to buy other lands in the area until he had accumulated 2,332 acres, including most of the area between the hills at the head of Cayuga Lake.

Simeon DeWitt's role in the founding and establishment of Ithaca would prove to be of lasting significance. It is said that he named the central settlement of the township of Ulysses for the Greek island Ithakē, which in his imagination resembled our region and because it was the central spot in the life of the hero Odysseus, whose Roman name was Ulysses. Although DeWitt was not able to make Ithaca his home until the very end of his life, he was its principal planner and caretaker. A map of 1807 (Map 2) shows that he had surveyed 49 lots, destined to be the heart of the settlement, and that parts of five streets had been plotted—Court Street (originally called Mill Street), North Aurora, Tioga, Seneca, and Buffalo (then called Buell). The center of the settlement was the block on North Aurora between Seneca and Buffalo, and the locations of the first buildings were probably determined by the mill site on Cascadilla Creek.

DeWitt let the lots out (on a one-year lease) to people who would husband the land and the community. He designated areas for orchards and fruit trees; he set aside timber reserves and a lot for a school site. He sold lots to certain enterprises for specific purposes; lot #71, for example, was sold to the Bank of Newburgh in 1815 for a branch office. He envisioned the arrangement of the town's center and the nature of its commerce. Many of his plans for the village were not carried out, for after his death much of his land was put on the market, sold in parcels, and dispersed. (Most of the original Bloodgood tract was acquired eventually by C. M. Titus and John McGraw, of whom we shall hear later.) Even so, the very orderly layout of downtown Ithaca (compare it on a map with the arrangement of the village of Cayuga Heights, for example), the location of the business district, and the major impetus for the settlement's early growth, all came from DeWitt. He supported the building of the Clinton House, in which he lived for the last three years of his life and in which he died. He backed the Ithaca & Owego Railroad, pledged credit to it, heralded it as a great potential success. In that he was wrong, for the financial crash three years after his death destroyed that particular development dream. In his faith in Ithaca, however, he was not wrong. As early as 1810, he saw it as a very important place: "Its advantages and situation cannot fail of giving it a rapid growth and making it one of the first inland places of trade."[3]

Simeon DeWitt was indeed a man of vision and imagination, and it was his enthusiasm that carried the young community along. To us today the Ithaca of 1810 would not have seemed particularly promising, although by that time it already had—according to DeWitt's own description—a three-story hotel, five two-story houses, and thirty frame dwellings of one story, as well as a schoolhouse and buildings for a phenomenal variety of commercial establishments: carpenters, cabinetmakers, blacksmiths, coopers, tanners, as well as shoemakers, tailors, hatters, two lawyers, a doctor, a watch cleaner, and a miller. There were also some taverns and a public library. The change was indeed considerable from the six houses or so scattered over the site in 1798. By the time the county was established in 1817, Ithaca also had several gristmills (which ground coarse grain used for feed), flouring mills, a plaster mill, and a sawmill. And there was a good deal of business and trade in potash, salt, grain, and cattle. In 1815, however, most of what is now the city was only partly cleared or was simply wilderness.

While the central community of Ulysses Township (#22 of the Military Tract) was getting its start, other areas in the region were being settled, and the turn of the century saw the beginnings of the county's major towns and villages. The earliest settlement was in the northwestern corner of the county, where around 1790 Samuel Weyburn built a cabin at Taughannock Point (called Goodwin's Point, and a stopping place for travelers). Then Abner Treman (or Truman) drew military lot #2 and came in March 1793 to settle the area around the village of Trumansburg, which bears his name today. Lansing (then called Milton) was first settled in 1791, when two brothers named Silas and Henry Ludlow from Athens on the Susquehanna came north from Ithaca on the ice of Cayuga Lake (in February); they were followed by the Bloom family and Andrew Myers and within a few years there were several groups of houses.

Beginnings and the Early Years

The town of Caroline saw its earliest pioneers in 1795; Captain David Rich came from western Massachusetts to build a log house, and a week later a widow named Maria Earsley arrived from New Jersey with five sons and four daughters. The first to stay in Danby arrived there in the same year; they were the Yaples and the Dumonds, the early settlers of Ithaca. The first settler of Military Township #23, Dryden (which already had a road running through it in 1795), was Amos Sweet, who in 1797 put up a ten-foot-square log house that was converted into a schoolhouse in 1804. In the fall of 1798 three families settled Willow Glen, among them Captain George Robertson, who was the first resident freeholder, the first supervisor, and the first innkeeper of the town. John Perrin from western Massachusetts settled on lot #75 in the town of Locke (Military Township #18, from which Groton was formed), a lot belonging to Major Benjamin Hicks of Canajoharie, built a house, and spent the winter of 1797/8 there. In 1798 Jabez Hanner settled on the Ulysses-Enfield line and several years later, in 1804, the Judah Baker family built a house in Enfield and became its first permanent residents. The last township of the county to be settled was Newfield; it was in 1800 that James Thomas came to the area called Poney Hollow (a shortened version of Saponey Hollow, so called for the Catawban Indian tribe, the Saponeys, who had lived there). In 1802 Eliaken Dean with his family built on the west branch of the Inlet Creek because of the waterpower there; he purchased the land including the site of the present Newfield and called the settlement Florence. Newfield was originally part of Tioga County and in 1811 was given the name of Cayuta.

In the early days these various settlements all developed in much the same way. There were many scattered small groups of buildings, usually strung along the banks of the creeks of the region. The water supplied power for the mills—gristmills, plaster mills, sawmills—and every community had at least one. Initially, log cabins were built, but pioneers soon replaced them with frame houses. The settlements had taverns, general stores, a schoolhouse (one schoolhouse for every settlement), and at least one church organization. Every community had its government, the settlers having brought a knowledge of civic structure with them from their original locales, mainly New England, New Jersey, Virginia, Pennsylvania, and areas to the east in New York State. Early officials of the settlements attended to the basic civil needs of the communities and, in a number of cases, to social services as well. Certain communities developed industries and services very early, but the major occupation of the settlers was farming.

Travel was difficult for the early settlers, although provisions were made for roads from the beginning. The first road in the county came into existence in 1791 when legislative enactment opened the right-of-way between Virgil (in Cortland County) and Ludlowville. In 1795 the road was cut from Virgil to Ithaca by way of Dryden and for years was called the Bridle Road—it was so narrow that riders had to lead their horses by the bridle where the bushes were too thick. A charter was granted by the state legislature in 1804 for the Bath & Jericho (now Bainbridge) Turnpike and the road was laid out through Caroline, Dryden, Ithaca, Enfield, Hector, and on westward. This road came to be known as the Catskill Turnpike and was a very early stagecoach route; for years it was the leading road of the region. In 1811 the Ithaca & Owego Turnpike and the Ithaca & Geneva Turnpike were both finished, the former having been built on the old trail that the earliest settlers had traveled to the head of Cayuga Lake.

The state granted charters to private companies for the construction of these roads as the most practical means of opening the wilderness to settlement, and the roads were operated as toll roads. The only road between the east and west sides of the valley at the head of Cayuga Lake was called Five Mile Drive, and it was passable only when the weather was dry. Travel on these pioneer roads was anything but comfortable; after the frost had gone out of the ground, the roads were paths of mud, with stumps and boulders everywhere. As a result pioneers often moved in the winter. There were stretches of "corduroy" road, where logs were laid crosswise over swampy places so that horses and vehicles could pass. Often the roads were driven through dense forest, and yet people persevered and came on through the wilderness.

The early residents of our region were hardworking people whose daily life involved hardships, long hours of toil, and very few comforts. Most were engaged in or depended upon a rather

Beginnings and the Early Years

4. Daniel D. Tompkins (1774–1825). Governor of New York from 1807 to 1817, he was inaugurated on March 4, 1817, as the nation's sixth vice-president and served two terms under President James Monroe.

primitive agriculture that yielded hogs, cattle, horses, and poultry as well as grains, common vegetables, fruits, dairy products, and maple sugar. They also produced flax, timber, and potash. Most family members worked together on the farms, for the growing and harvesting of the crops was everyone's job. In addition the pioneer man would work as a woodsman, builder, woodworker; he slaughtered animals, smoked the hides, tanned leather, prepared flax, made maple sugar and cider. The pioneer woman's job was to organize and run a household that on the average consisted of six people; the kitchen with its large cooking fireplace was the center of her world. She tended the fire, cooked, baked, preserved fruits

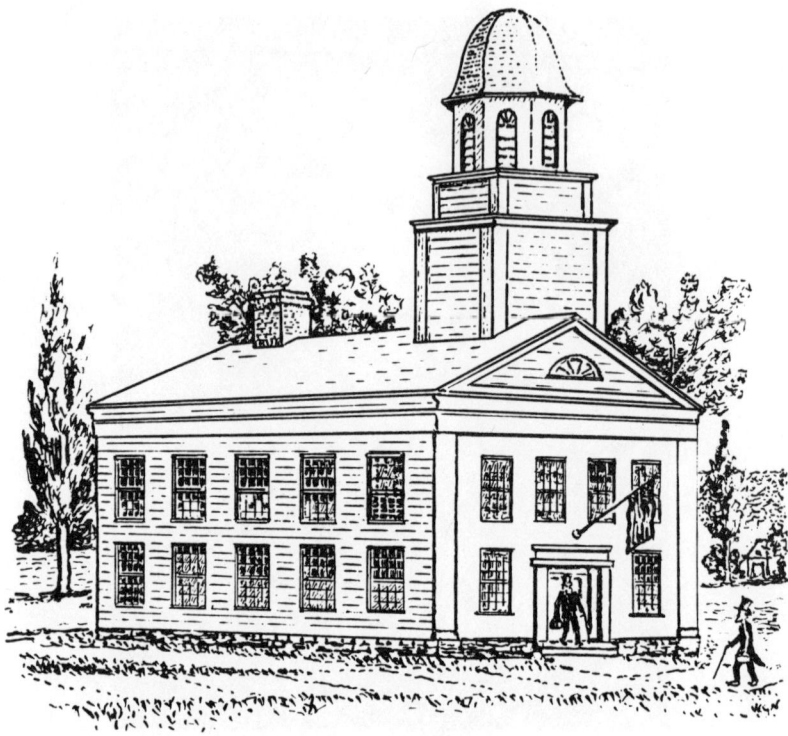

5. First Tompkins County Courthouse. This wooden structure, built on land given to the county by Simeon DeWitt, was replaced in 1854 by the present Old County Courthouse at 121 East Court Street (figure 92).

and vegetables; she also made clothes and soap and did the washing and ironing. And, of course, she raised the children, supervising their various tasks and occupations, teaching them their book learning (because for most farm children there was formal schooling only sporadically, during the winter months), and their lessons in manners and survival.

Tompkins County came into being through an act of the state legislature passed on April 17, 1817. The county was created from parts of Cayuga and Seneca counties and comprised the military townships of Ulysses, Hector, and Dryden, and sections of Locke and Milton (also military townships), plus parts of what is now the city of Ithaca. In 1822 the towns of Caroline, Danby, and Cayuta (now Newfield) were annexed from Tioga County. In 1853 part of the town of Newfield was annexed to Chemung County. The town of Hector, which originally had come from Seneca County, was part of Tompkins County until 1854, when it was moved to Schuyler County. The new county was named for Daniel E. Tompkins (1774-1825, figure 4), who as governor of New York State from 1807 to 1817 had proved an extremely able administrator, particularly during the very unpopular War of 1812. A man of great strength and vision in time of war—both with the English and in the form of domestic political skirmishes—he had just been inaugurated as sixth vice-president of the United States in the administration of James Monroe. The act of the legislature organizing the county designated Ithaca (then a community of about 400 residents) as the county seat. It required the new county to convey a site for the county buildings, appoint supervisors, and pay a security of $7000. Failure to do so would have meant reannexation to the counties of Cayuga and Seneca. The provisions were quickly met, however; in 1818 a wooden building housing a courthouse and jail was hastily erected and made ready for use (figure 5). The first officials of the county, appointed in 1817, were a judge, surrogate, clerk, sheriff, and district attorney. The clerk's office, a small one-story brick building with a brick floor, was located on Tioga Street. The first Board of Supervisors of the county convened in 1817. Tompkins County was officially in existence.

[2]

Growth and Development: The Communities

IN April 1817, when Tompkins County was organized, it got the towns of Hector and Ulysses (and Covert for two years) from Seneca County, Dryden and parts of Locke and Genoa—which soon became Division (later Groton) and Lansing—from Cayuga County. The village of Ithaca, although it was not incorporated until several years later, was named the county seat. The original boundaries were retained until March 22, 1822, when the towns of Caroline, Danby, and Cayuta (Newfield)—which were not part of the Military Tract—were annexed from Tioga County. A section of Newfield and the village of Hector became parts of Chemung and Schuyler counties respectively in the 1850s. Of the original towns, there remain today nine—Caroline, Danby, Dryden, Enfield, Groton, Ithaca, Lansing, Newfield, Ulysses—and they contain the city of Ithaca, six incorporated villages—Cayuga Heights, Dryden, Freeville, Groton, Lansing, Trumansburg—and numerous smaller communities. Newfield incorporated as a village in 1895 but dissolved its charter in 1925 and remains unincorporated to this day. The county has an area of 580 square miles.

Throughout Tompkins County's history, Ithaca has been far and away the largest and most vital community and the focus of the county's services. In the nineteenth century it was the transportation center, the main location for business and industry, and in 1888 became the county's only city. It retains its prominent place today, as the seat of government and of the county's important organizations: the hospital (which is now privately owned and operated), the public library, the historical society, the principal churches, and the largest institution, Cornell University. The county airport is just over the town line in Lansing. Because of its geographical situation at the head of the lake and near the county's territorial center, Ithaca is easily accessible from all parts of the county.

The early administration of the county must have been somewhat vague and arbitrary. There were a courthouse and a jail, and there undoubtedly were certain legal disputes to be settled, mostly over conflicting land claims and bogus titles. The early toll roads, chartered to private companies by the state, fairly soon were turned over to the county. Very early (in 1827) the Board of Supervisors voted to erect a poorhouse; a wooden building was put up in the town of Ulysses, about four miles from Ithaca. In 1876 it housed 75 people, and the population listings of the year 1877 note 454 county paupers.

Through the years, with the growth of population and its attendant expansion of industry, buildings, and services, the responsibilities of the county administration have increased enormously. Following World War II and the Korean conflict, the county was to experience the greatest growth in its history, and since that time several specific issues have arisen, among them the new hospital facility and its transferal to private ownership, the management of the airport, the new public library building, and the continual need for improved transportation routes.

Through the years the county and its communities have dealt with some perennial problems. The terrain, with its hills and many bodies of water, has been probably the largest factor in the county's development. The hills, with all their beauty, are hazardous, especially in winter, and their steepness has caused many terrible truck and car accidents, colossal obstacles to road and railroad building, and other problems of communication. And through the years, again and again one reads accounts of floods—floods that have devastated entire communities (figures 6 and 35). Not until the beginning of the present century were measures taken to alleviate the problems brought on, especially in Ithaca, by the spring

6. Ithaca Fairground (September 10, 1890). Often through the years the low areas in the county have stood under water. Many of the fairground's pavilions are visible, but one wonders about an event involving a half-submerged horse and buggy!

(and sometimes the fall) floods. The county has also had its share of fires, financial crises brought on by great booms of speculation and investment, and of course wartime vicissitudes. Through these events the residents have shown themselves to be determined, courageous, and highly adaptable.

Ithaca

As the county's only city, Ithaca stands first in this historical sketch of the different communities within Tompkins County. On March 16, 1821, an act of the state legislature divided the township of Ulysses into the current Ulysses, Enfield, and a town with the

Growth and Development: The Communities

name of Ithaca. The village of this new town was incorporated on April 2, 1821, and a Board of Trustees was elected. Daniel Bates, the operator of a tannery and a man noted for his thrift (he had the habit of jingling coins from hand to hand because he enjoyed the music they made), was named the first president for a one-year term. At that time the village had about 1,000 inhabitants.

Among the first ordinances passed were measures to prevent domestic animals, mainly pigs and horses, from running free in the streets; people were forbidden to discharge firearms or set off rockets, nor could one fly a kite or play ball in either of the two main streets (called Owego and Aurora streets). A speed limit was set on horse-drawn carriages. Residents were required to pay for a water supply in case of fire, and each dwelling was to have an adequate ladder and leather buckets in proportion to the number of fireplaces. In July 1824 the trustees were empowered to build and regulate a public market, and in the next month a 24-foot square building was erected at the corner of Tioga and Green streets in which market was held every day except Sunday. A fire company had been organized in 1823 and by 1863 the village had seven companies; in 1871 fifteen companies incorporated as the Ithaca Fire Department.

The village grew and prospered. More mills were built and operated on Cascadilla Creek and on Fall Creek, just over the village line. Several banks got charters, church buildings went up, hotels and taverns were built, sidewalks were graded and graveled. The public square (DeWitt Park) owned by the Presbyterian Church was beautified and improvements were made in the waterworks. By 1830 the village had 3,592 inhabitants, four schools, and three newspapers. Yet even with all this progress, life could be grim; about half the population suffered each year from malaria or fever and ague, the churches were said to be dreary and dismal, and there was mud everywhere. When the lake was high in the spring, the whole western end of Owego (now State) Street was impassable. School teachers were usually uncultured, occasionally uneducated, and often brutal. But amid the hardship, discomfort, and dirt were perseverance and great accomplishment.

Ithaca by the early 1830s was the transportation center of the county and a bustling, growing community. Stagecoach routes from Catskill and Jersey City, from Albany, Auburn, Geneva, and Elmira, all passed through the village. The steamboat *DeWitt Clinton* departed at 6 A.M. daily except Sunday, with scheduled arrival at noon at Cayuga Bridge (a wooden structure that spanned the northern end of the lake) and return to Ithaca by sunset; it carried 50 to 60 passengers a day on the round trip. Eight or so canal boats moved up and down the lake, hauling lumber, potash, flour, salt, and plaster. Charters had been granted for five separate railroad companies to build lines to and through the village. It was an exciting time in Ithaca's history; prospects were bright after the completion of the Erie Canal for Ithaca to become a great canal and railroad center, an inland metropolis. In 1830 the Clinton House (figures 38 and 87), one of the finest and most elegant hotels west of New York City, opened its doors, and in 1834 the first train of cars traveled from Ithaca to Owego. Land prices went up in this era of wild speculation. One piece of the Simeon DeWitt estate, for example, selling in January 1836 for $4,676, was bought in July for $52,929. Then came the national financial panic of 1837, business projects came to a standstill, wages were drastically reduced. The village ran into debt and taxes were increased (though collecting them was difficult).

In the years between 1842 and 1852 came a return to economic stability, and a man named Ezra Cornell (who in 1828 had come to find work in Ithaca) was contracted to lay telegraph wire for Samuel F. B. Morse. In 1843 the Old City Hall was put up on the corner of Seneca and Tioga Streets, for over a century this handsome Greek Revival structure served the community, first as Village Hall and later as City Hall (see figures 10 and 93). During the 1850s more churches were built, and the Civil War years saw great prosperity for the region, which benefited from the business of transporting war supplies. In 1863 Ezra Cornell provided funds for a library, a three-story structure on Seneca and Tioga streets. And in the late 1860s came the founding of Cornell University, a monumental event in the history of Ithaca, of all Tompkins County in fact. With the establishment and growth of the university came a renewed expansion of Ithaca and its environs. Shortly thereafter came another wave of railroad-building projects, most of which also failed, bringing financial ruin upon many investors, among them Ezra Cornell.

Growth and Development: The Communities

The village of Ithaca had grown to 5,685 inhabitants at the end of the Civil War. It was not a very beautiful place in 1865, although lush shade trees in summer offered cool greenery. Most of the houses were wooden; there were a few grand houses (among them the stately "Three Sisters" in the 200 block of North Geneva Street, of which two are still standing). An English visitor described them as "domestic architecture which presents the front of a Doric temple with family and culinary developments in the rear."[4] The Boardman House, another imposing residence still standing, was built in 1864 (figure 7). Much of the central business district was developed in the 1860s and 1870s; a significant number of "blocks" were erected to accommodate various commercial enterprises. The old Ithaca Hotel, a three-story wooden structure built in 1809 by Luther Gere (he had put up Ithaca's first public house in 1805, see figure 8), burned in 1871, in a major fire that destroyed eleven buildings on State Street, and was rebuilt as a four-story brick building in 1872. In that same year the city's oldest business, *The Ithaca Journal*, put up its own building, the Journal Block, located on South Tioga Street behind the Wilgus Block (figure 9). The local streets were numbered in 1867, and street signs were posted. The name of Owego Street was changed to State Street, and in 1870 an iron bridge was constructed across Six Mile Creek at Aurora Street. The Presbyterian Church spire dominated the village, as had the church's hellfire and brimstone preacher, the Reverend William Wisner, a man of ardor, conviction, and devotion—a power for sinners to reckon with.

With the expansion of Cornell University and its need for services came a rapid growth of the village. By 1880 there were 9,105 inhabitants, living mostly between Farm and Green streets to the north and south, and the West End and Aurora Street to the west and east (figure 10). The business area developed on Aurora and State streets chiefly, extending south to Six Mile Creek. A few houses dotted West Hill while more were built on East Hill; a great number of them served as student rooming houses. The flats south of Green and west of Cayuga streets were swamps. One block of State Street was paved, and part of Aurora Street was planked; otherwise the roads and streets were dirt, and in the spring they became avenues of mud. The water company dug a new reservoir in 1875 to supplement the small "lower" reservoir near the railroad

7. Boardman House. Built in 1866, this residence in DeWitt Park was first a private home, then the administration building for the Ithaca Conservatory of Music (later Ithaca College). Recently renovated, it serves as an office building today. See also figure 53.

incline up South Hill, and by 1878 the first telephones had been hooked up. In 1875 two Physics professors at Cornell, William Anthony and George Moler, built an electric dynamo to demonstrate uses of electrical power at the Centennial Exposition in Philadelphia. At Cornell it provided current for the first outdoor electric lights in America: two arc lights in the towers of McGraw Hall and Sage Chapel, which by 1880 gave out intense light visible for miles around. By 1884 Ithaca had seventy arc streetlights, operating on the rather unreliable "moonlight schedule"—that is, service was not provided on nights when the Almanac predicted

8. Ithaca Hotel. Shown here in an 1841 engraving by Henry Walton, the hotel was a stop on the Catskill Turnpike. The stagecoach office was next door and, next to it, L. Atwater's grocery store.

that the moon would shine. This progress was only relative, however; during his term as village president in 1877, industrialist Joseph B. Sprague was active in having cows removed from the city streets.

Ithaca in the 1880s began to reflect its considerable prosperity nonetheless with a look of wealth and elegance (figure 11). The business section of the city on State and North Aurora streets had been built up, especially in the 1870s, with large, solid commercial

9. Wilgus Block, Ithaca (c. 1895). Built in 1868 by the Wilgus brothers, the building had a department store on the first floor (Rothschild's moved there in 1889) and the Wilgus Opera House on the third and fourth floors. At the time of this picture the Ithaca Conservatory of Music occupied the second and third floors. The Journal Block behind the Wilgus Block was built in 1872. To the right is the Sprague Block, built in 1870.

blocks; more would be added in the following years. Certain residential sections of the village had large and gracious mansions; the 300 block of East Court Street (on the south side) saw four Italianate houses built in the 1860s and 1870s, and rows of beautiful homes lined the 300 and 400 blocks of North Aurora, North Tioga, and North Cayuga streets and the streets to the south and

Growth and Development: The Communities

10. Seneca Street and East Hill. Taken in 1868, this picture shows Cascadilla Hall and the just completed Morrill Hall on the hill, the Village (later City) Hall, and several residences. The white building to the left is the Cascadilla Mills.

west of DeWitt Park. Considerable building on the hills, especially around the university, included many faculty houses; although called "cottages," many were simply grandiose.

One architect played a particularly prominent role in the appearance of the village. He was William Henry Miller (1848–1922), and between 1870 and 1920 he designed more than seventy buildings in Ithaca and its environs. On the Cornell campus he was responsible for Barnes, Stimson, and Risley halls and the Uris Library and was one of three architects to work on the Andrew Dickson White House. Down in the village his work was extensive; among his designs were several commercial blocks,

[47]

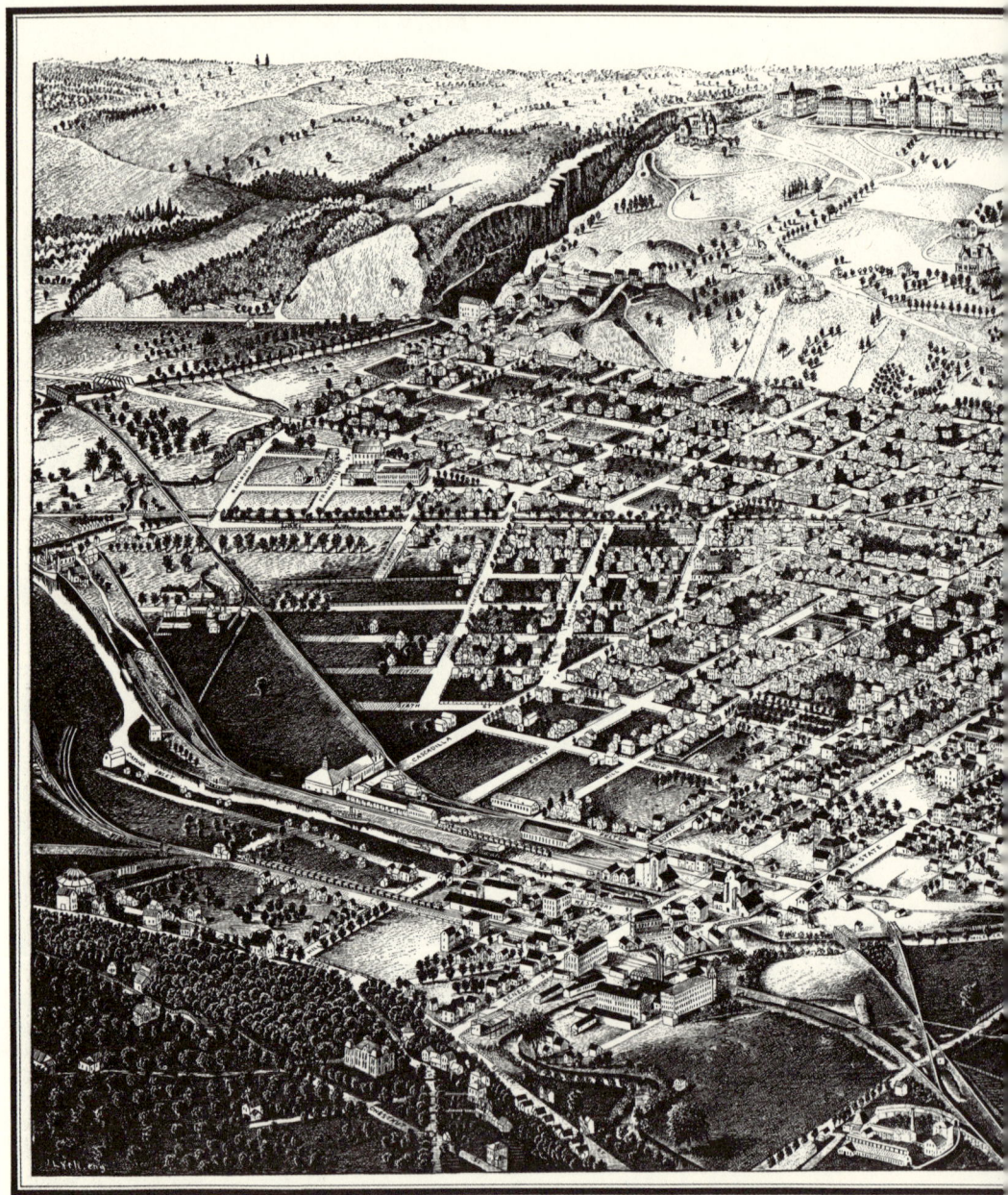

11. Ithaca in 1882. This bird's eye view shows the extent of the village, with its factories, railroads, fairground, and residences (including the McGraw-Fiske mansion at the top). To the extreme left, at the junction of

the Inlet and Cascadilla Creek, is the steamboat landing (figure 74). The small "lower" reservoir is visible to the right, next to the railroad incline up South Hill.

12. Cornell University (c. 1880). In the foreground is Sage Chapel with Morrill, McGraw, and White halls (the "Stone Row") beyond. Facing south are Franklin (*left*) and Sibley (*right*). The McGraw-Fiske mansion with its spectacular setting and views is in the background to the left. For other views of Cornell University, see figures 49, 50, 51, 76, 77, and 82.

the Second Empire alteration of the Clinton House, the high school building, three churches, and several residences. Miller's most splendid accomplishments, however, were the two Sage mansions (built in 1877 next to each other on East Hill between State and Seneca streets), the reconstruction of John McGraw's house by his third wife, Jane, on South Hill (originally built in 1850 and called Terrace Hill, figure 60), and the palatial McGraw-Fiske mansion, built for Jennie McGraw Fiske on a thirty-acre site at the southwest corner of the Cornell campus (figure 12). Designed to resemble a Loire Valley chateau, it commanded dramatic vistas of the lake, the valley, and the Fall Creek gorge.[5]

Growth and Development: The Communities

13. Labor Day Parade (1890). Two years after its charter, the city of Ithaca held its first Labor Day parade, shown here on Aurora Street (not yet paved) between Seneca and State streets. In the background is the Tompkins House, and on the floats are Aurora Street businessmen.

In the year 1888 Ithaca was chartered as a city, a great event that culminated seven years of controversy and three different versions of the charter. This last was described as a "formidable document" containing, in the words of the *Syracuse Herald*, "sufficient redundant English to do for a city the size of London. There are 217 sections." The *New York Herald Tribune* sent along its congratulations to Ithaca with a pious wish: "May she manage to keep her streets and Board of Eldermen clean, her standard of public sentiment high, and her taxes low." Ithaca's cityhood was celebrated on June 1, 1888, with an 8-page special issue of the newspaper, a 29-gun salute, bells and whistles, and a special program provided by the merchants on Aurora Street, which scheduled band music, speeches, fireworks, and several different periods of "noise" (see figure 13).

Ithaca's last president and first mayor was David B. Stewart, a cigar maker and wholesale grocer. Under the new charter the president became mayor, trustees became aldermen, and the Board of Trustees became Common Council. An iron bridge across the Cascadilla Gorge extended Factory Street on East Hill (see figure 46), opening up a large tract for development to the north, and Common Council changed the name of the street to Stewart Avenue—much to the annoyance of many city people who considered the Stewarts upstarts (the family had come from Newfield only twenty-one years before) and saw the land-development scheme and Stewart's priority to install sewers somewhat differently than their plans for expensive brick streets. A more general problem that affected the people's judgment of the parvenu Stewart and his successors was that it cost much more to operate a community under a city charter than it did a simple village. New offices had to be created, with the necessary salaries attached. The city charter was revised in 1909 when permanent boards were established, and again in 1931 to set the mayor's salary at $2,500 a year. The first paid mayor was the Swedish engineer Herman Bergholtz, who had come to Ithaca in 1892 to expand the electric trolley system and who had also worked on the design and arrangement of Stewart Park. Other changes over the years have been in the establishment of a zoning system in 1923 and a department of finance with a city comptroller in the late 1960s. In 1975 a commission was appointed to draft a new city charter; its proposal for a mayor-council-administrator form of government was turned down by the voters.

Two floods in the winter of 1901/2 moved citizens to action on the problem of the spring floods. The state proposed building a new barge canal along the route of the old Erie Canal; Ithacans felt improving the outlet would help in flood control and gave their support to Albany. Nothing happened until another flood in June 1905 moved the legislature to fund the improvement of the Cayuga-Seneca Canal and thus create an adequate outlet for water from the lake. Provisions were also made for control of the creeks and drainage of swamp lands. The Inlet was widened and deepened, embankments along Fall Creek and the lower part of Six Mile Creek were built up; new bridges were built. With a new

Growth and Development: The Communities

channel for the Inlet (which was redug and redirected again in the late 1960s as the flood control channel), much swamp was filled and the residential area extended to the park region at the head of the lake. Washington Park was filled in and developed in 1908 and Stewart Park developed as a city recreational area in the 1920s.

In the 1960s and 1970s came an era of urban development and restoration, and with it the building of the Ithaca Commons and the establishment of the DeWitt Park Historical District. In this era, too, came the irrevocable destruction of certain buildings that, though not financial successes perhaps, were of considerable sentimental and historical value. Among them were the Old City Hall (figure 93) and the Ithaca Hotel, the first replaced by a parking garage, the second demolished to create an empty space at State and Aurora streets, which was filled only years afterward. The Clinton House, which had survived several fires and transformations (including conversion to Second Empire style complete with mansard roof), ceased business as a hotel in 1973 and was purchased that year by Historic Ithaca. After complete renovation and the addition of an outside elevator and stair tower on the Seneca Street side (a large community restoration project directed by Historic Ithaca), it is now occupied by the DeWitt Historical Society, retail businesses, offices, and Historic Ithaca. The old high school building, having served in several different educational capacities, was privately developed as a basement mall, with offices and apartments on the upper floors. The Boardman House, after standing unused for many years and the object of almost endless controversy, has also been developed privately and today houses office space. The Henry St. John school building has been converted to apartments.

The Ithaca Commons has been an admirable and highly successful urban renewal project, one that has brought the city national attention. The planners got considerable input about the project from businesses, public agencies, and private citizens and then went on in 1974 to build the first such pedestrian mall in New York State. The cost of the project was split between the public and private sectors. The creation of the mall involved closing off the two blocks of State Street to vehicular traffic, plantings, de-

14. Mills in Free Hollow (Forest Home). The mill in the foreground made cider.

signing and equipping recreational areas, and renovating buildings. The Commons has become the focus for many downtown commercial and recreational activities.

Other communities outside the city but part of the town of Ithaca include Renwick Heights—part of the original Renwick Tract and developed after 1900, but never consolidated within the city—and Forest Home, originally called Free Hollow, on Fall Creek (figure 14). One of the county's first mills was built there already in 1794; over the years it had a powder mill, a woodworking factory in operation for almost one hundred years, and a factory built by Arnold McIntyre which manufactured telescopes and firearms. Levi Coon built a small shed and a triphammer near the present Triphammer Bridge and produced some of the finest guns

Growth and Development: The Communities

in northeastern United States. The triphammer pounded away rhythmically at the foot of the falls; people came to watch it work. Triphammer Road, which starts above the bridge, was named for it.

Beyond the northeastern border of the city lies Cayuga Heights, a village incorporated in 1915, when it had a population of 137. It has known steady growth since then, and in 1954 its boundaries were expanded to include the newly developed areas to the northeast. In that same year the villagers voted against annexation by the city and drew up plans to build their own sewer system to accommodate an ever growing population. The village's volunteer Fire Department has been a model for other communities and has given prominent service to the village as well as to adjacent areas in Lansing and Ithaca.

Caroline

From the early 1800s the town of Caroline, located in the southeast corner of the county, has had the largest number of independent small settlements of any town in the county, many of them surviving today. Lacking any incorporated village, Caroline has nonetheless been important in the county's transportation story: one of the early main roads—the Catskill Turnpike (now Route 79)—as well as a major railroad traversed the township.

Caroline. The first settler in the town, according to most reports, was Captain David Rich. He came from western Massachusetts in 1795 and built a log house; the first recorded deed of settlement is in his name. The previous year, however, a widow named Maria Earsley had set out on horseback from New Jersey with her oldest son and her brother, found the land she liked, and purchased one hundred acres at $3 per acre. She went back to prepare her family for the move; in the fall of 1794 her son returned and built a log cabin. In March of 1795, a week after Captain Rich's arrival, Mrs. Earsley came back to Caroline with her large family. For several years the Earsleys and Captain Rich were the only settlers. In 1804 and 1805 a group came from southern Maryland and Virginia, bringing their slaves with them and keeping them until the state abolished slavery in 1827. Among these settlers was Joseph Speed, a medical doctor who was interested in benevolence, the colonization of emancipated slaves, and the temperance movement. His brother John Jacob Speed settled nearby, and later their cousins John James and William built several houses and mills and opened a store. John Jacob Speed also had the postoffice on the turnpike with the name Speedsville, and there was also the Speed tavern (figure 39). The Speeds' settlement was called The City; Caroline was also called the Yankee Settlement, because many of the early settlers had come from New England.

Brooktondale. General John Cantine, who had been both a state assemblyman and senator, had been appointed a commissioner in 1788 to settle land disputes along the Susquehanna, Chemung, and Tioga rivers. In 1792 he acquired 32,000 acres in the Six Mile Creek valley. He parceled out this land and encouraged people to settle it. He offered his son a piece on Six Mile Creek, and in 1798 John Jr. came and built a log cabin. In 1800 General Cantine sent six men to build a gristmill on the creek's north bank. In charge of the group was millwright Benoni Mulks, who followed the creek upstream and saw some promising land near the present village of Slaterville. Mulks's son John purchased a parcel of it from General Cantine in 1800 and built a cabin there the same year. The general had two mills and the first frame house in the community; dating from 1804, it was called the Mansion House. He also brought several slaves with him, who were freed in 1808 by the terms of his will.

Although General Cantine did buy and sell considerable land in the region, William Mott II did much more to settle the village. He bought out the Cantine mills and opened a general store; he then built additional mills and helped families to clear and farm the land. For a time he lived in the Mansion House, and it was through his influence that the settlement came to be called Mott's Corners. A school and several churches were built, and a woolen factory as well. By 1866 the community was thriving with several different industries, including a woolen mill that made socks and mittens and provided employment for about thirty-five people.

Growth and Development: The Communities

15. Brooktondale (c. 1890). The railroad trestle over Six Mile Creek (also in figure 42) is visible in the background.

The name was changed in 1882 first to Bridgeton and then to Brookton (in 1926 it would become Brooktondale because of continual postal confusion with Brockton, N.Y.). In 1884 the community had a roller skating rink. A railroad—originally the Utica, Ithaca & Elmira—ran through the lower end of the village and crossed Six Mile Creek on an old wooden trestle made of foot-square timbers (figure 15). In 1894 the wooden structure was replaced with a steel bridge, a procedure accomplished with no interruption of service. At the end of the trestle stood the Brookton station. The railroad, eventually purchased by the Lehigh Valley, was abandoned in 1935; the trestle was taken down and the metal salvaged for scrap.

Slaterville. In 1800 Richard Bush and two others came from Marbletown in Ulster County; Bush built a large square log house and opened a tavern, which was known for years as the Old Bush Stand. In the same year Levi Slater came to the area with General Cantine, borrowed his instruments, and surveyed the land, which he then purchased from the general. Returning the following year, he settled in what is now Slaterville. Levi Slater became the first town clerk of Caroline in 1811 and was captain of the Caroline Company during the War of 1812. He also owned the first distillery in the community. His brother Thomas settled nearby and opened a store; the community that grew up around it was called the Dutch Settlement because so many pioneers had come originally from Ulster County, itself first settled mainly by Dutch immigrants. John Robinson, who had come with Levi Slater, held the town's first school in the back of his home. Somewhat later, in 1819, Lyman Cobb, while teaching at a log schoolhouse on the Mulks farm, compiled and published in 1819 the first edition of his famous *Cobb's Spelling-Book*. The Reformed Dutch Church put up a two-story structure in Slaterville in 1820—the slaves of the congregation sat in the balcony.

With the building of mills, the church, and a store, the little village grew and the post office was established in 1823. The community had its greatest prosperity, however, after the discovery of the Magnetic Springs in 1871; the water, which contained many minerals, was believed to have curative properties. As watering spas had become particularly fashionable, Slaterville became a resort and its name was changed to Slaterville Springs. People came from all over the country to take the waters. Two hotels, the Magnetic Springs House and the Fountain House (figure 16) flourished; as many as two hundred summer guests at a time stayed in the village. During this period a stage operated between Slaterville and Ithaca; the business was sold in 1902, but for many years thereafter a service continued between Besemer Station and Slaterville.

Speedsville. This community, in the southeast corner of the town and the county, was settled by the Jenks family from Massachusetts in 1800. It was first called The Corners and then Jenksville but was finally named Speedsville with the establishment of the post office there in 1835, the result of a compromise between postmaster John J. Speed Jr. (the son of John Jacob Speed who had settled

Growth and Development: The Communities

16. Fountain House in Slaterville Springs. The hotel was built in 1872.

the Yankee Settlement)—a large and burly man who had long maintained a post office named Speedsville down the road and wanted the name kept—and the inhabitants of the community—who wanted the post office there (not down the road) and didn't care so much what name it had. Speedsville had a creamery and several cheese factories in the 1870s. In 1856 a covered wooden bridge was constructed over Boyer Creek (figure 17); it was replaced by a concrete structure in 1929.

In the town of Caroline are a number of other communities, including White Church, Caroline Center (so named for its central position in the town), Caroline Depot, Pugsley's Depot, Terryville (west of the Caroline Depot), and Besemer, a depot on the railroad built privately and named by Josiah Besemer, who wanted a station near the water tank there; it had a post office in 1876. Over the years the town had twenty-three mill sites along a seventeen-mile stretch of Six Mile Creek and its tributaries.

Caroline was set off from the town of Spencer and organized on February 22, 1811; the first town meeting was held at the Old Bush Stand. At this meeting the first officials were named: a supervisor, a town clerk, three commissioners of highways, a revenue collector, two overseers of the poor, two constables, two fence

17. Covered Bridge at Speedsville.

viewers, and a pondmaster. The 1820 census showed Tompkins County as having fifty slaves; thirty-two of them were in Caroline. Peter Webb, a former slave of John Jacob Speed, bought his freedom in 1818 (he had been purchased on the slave market at the age of thirteen for $90, the price being $1 per pound). His descendants settled in Ithaca.

A mystery surrounds the name of the town. Some reports say that it was picked at random from a spelling book and that Dr. Speed and General Cantine called their daughters Caroline after the town. Others say Dr. Speed named the town for his daughter Caroline.

Danby

The original settlers of the town of Danby came from Ithaca, where their claims to the land had proved invalid. They were seeking higher ground for their homes, away from the swampy area at the head of the lake. Isaac and John Dumond and Jacob and John

Yaple built in the north and northwestern parts of the town of Danby in the spring of 1795. They were followed by Dr. Lewis Beers and his brother Jabez, who arrived in 1797 from Connecticut. Dr. Beers was an active civic figure as the first justice of the peace, the first judge of the Court of Common Pleas, and the first (and only) president of the Ithaca & Owego Turnpike Company, which was in existence from 1812 until it surrendered the road to the state as a highway in 1841. He built the first frame house in the community in 1801 and in 1801/2 established the first post office. He was its postmaster for several years and constructed the town pound at his own expense (one-half of it was on a corner of his land). In addition to all this, Dr. Beers, who was of the Swedenborgian persuasion, found time to be founder and first pastor of the Church of New Jerusalem, which was organized in 1816 and became an important station on the Underground Railroad (figure 18).

Before the turn of the century the Dumonds and Yaples had built a sawmill and a gristmill on Buttermilk Creek, and a tannery was built in 1810. Another settlement called West Danby sprang up on the Inlet Creek, and it later became a depot for the Geneva, Ithaca & Sayre Railroad. This community did not have a store until the one built in 1850 by Ira Patchen, who operated it for more than thirty years. In 1936 the building was bought by the West Danby Grange, which had started in 1874. West Danby is an established community today with its own post office. Also in the town was South Danby, another small community. By 1830 the three hamlets had six church organizations and by 1865 a total of seventeen schools, of which fourteen were still open in 1931.

The town of Danby was formed from Spencer in 1811 and the first town meeting was held soon thereafter. It legally became part of Tompkins County in 1822. The name is believed to have come from a town in Vermont named in honor of the Earl of Danby. Outstanding features of the town are the Danby Federated Church, built in 1813 (figure 65), and the Danby Town Hall (figure 19), erected about 1826 and used as a Baptist church until 1866. It became the town hall in 1896; renovated in 1976 as a Bicentennial project, it houses the town offices and a meeting room. In front stands a 29-foot-tall Soldiers' Monument, of Italian marble

A Short History of Tompkins County

18. Village of Danby Today.

Growth and Development: The Communities

19. Danby Town Hall. This building was first a church, then the town hall. The Soldiers' Monument stands in front.

with a granite base, which lists the names, ages, and death dates of forty-five men who gave their lives to preserve the Union. Fund raising for the monument began in 1866 and over $1,900 was gathered by private efforts, including dramatic presentations (admission cost 10 cents) with such titles as "We're All Teetotalers," "Stagestruck Yankee," and "Popping the Question." Danby today has no industries except farming, and most of its residents work elsewhere in the region.

Dryden

The town of Dryden extends from near the center of the county to the eastern border and was #23 of the original townships in the Military Tract. It is one of the few towns in the county to retain its original dimensions (or nearly so; in 1886 seven lots were ceded to Caroline). Soldiers often resold their lots for very little; one lot, three miles west of Dryden Village and one-mile square, was sold for a coat, a hat, a drink of rum, and a dollar.

Before the arrival of the first settlers a road crossed the town from east to west, called the Bridle Road; built by the state, it was completed to Ithaca in 1795. In 1797 Amos Sweet, the first settler, put up a ten-foot-square log house in Dryden Village, a building that was converted into a schoolhouse in 1804. Three families settled the Willow Glen area just west of the village in the fall of 1798. Captain George Robertson, a young carpenter, came on foot and purchased lot #53 in 1797; he returned in March 1798 and planted seed grain. He harvested a good crop and thus was able to supply other settlers. He was also the town's first supervisor and operated the first tavern.

The town of Dryden merged with Township #22 (Ulysses) in 1794 and was set off again in 1803 (it would annex part of Danby in 1856); the first town meeting was held at the home of George Robertson. The post office was established about 1815; mail was carried on foot over the Bridle Road from Ithaca. The Eight-Square Schoolhouse, one of the county's landmarks, was built in 1827 (figure 20). Dryden became an incorporated village on the south branch of Fall Creek in 1857 and was reincorporated in 1865; Freeville, the township's other village, was incorporated in 1887. Other settlements in the town are Etna (which was on the line of the Utica, Ithaca & Elmira Railroad), Varna (on Fall Creek and also on the railroad line), and Ellis Hollow.

From its beginning the town of Dryden prospered. It had good soil, abundant waterpower, and large amounts of forest, particularly white pine. Lumbering was an early industry; the census of 1835 reported fifty-one sawmills in the town. There were also sulphur, magnesium, and iron springs west of the village and at one time Dryden had a sanatorium, with a doctor in charge. Over the years the town has been home to woolen mills, a leather manufactory, and a marble works.

For a while there was some question about whether the town's center should be at Willow Glen or at Dryden. In 1812 Edward Griswold gave a blacksmith forty acres of land to locate in Dryden;

Growth and Development: The Communities

20. Eight-Square Schoolhouse, Dryden.

he also set up a store on the northeast corner of the Dryden Four Corners, gave land to the Presbyterians for their church, and deeded one hundred acres to his son Abram, who then gave land to the villagers for a common. Thus was Griswold instrumental in establishing the site of the village. Another son, Edward, bought lot #50 in 1818 and started a farm, still in operation on the McClintock Road; his descendants, the Willard Downeys, live in the farmhouse though they have rented out the farm. Joseph McGraw settled on the southern hill between Dryden and Slaterville, in an area called the Irish Settlement. His son John, whose investments in western land were highly successful, acquired property in Ithaca, built a splendid mansion on South Hill, and made considerable gifts to Cornell University. John's daughter, Jennie, not only gave Cornell its chimes mechanism but provided Dryden with its library, naming it Southworth Library for her mother's family (see figure 59).

The Dryden Agricultural Society was organized in 1856 and established permanent grounds on East Main Street. The village's fair house, an unusual twelve-sided structure, became a model for

21. Dryden Fair. Except for Dryden's unusual fair building, this is a typical fair scene in the county toward the end of the nineteenth century.

fairs in the west (figure 21). For years the Dryden Fair was considered the largest and best in the state; the last fair was held there in 1917, and the building was torn down in 1933. Today Dryden is the location of two of the county's important educational institutions—Tompkins Cortland Community College (known by all as TC3) and the George Junior Republic.

The village of Freeville was first settled by Daniel White, who came in 1798 and built a gristmill there. The community grew and by 1900 it had 440 residents. At that time four passenger trains met at the Freeville junction three times a day; express and baggage as well as passengers were exchanged in a period of twenty minutes (figure 22).

One of the town's outstanding early settlers was John Ellis, who arrived in 1798 with his brother Peleg. John Ellis became a judge and a member of the state legislature; for twenty-six years he was

Growth and Development: The Communities

22. Freeville Junction. During the heyday of the railroads one could take trains here to go in any of four directions.

state supervisor. He came to be known throughout the region as the "King of Dryden." His brother had exchanged property in Herkimer County for lot #84 in Dryden, the locality now known as Ellis Hollow. Captain George Robertson helped him to locate his lot and clear the land. Ellis built a log house at the headwaters of Cascadilla Creek; his homestead, called Headwaters and modified over the years, still stands on Ellis Hollow Road and is known as the Myers-Ellis house. A road was cleared from Ithaca east to lot #71 in 1799 by Zephaniah Brown; he and Ellis then cleared the road on to Ellis Hollow in 1801. Peleg Ellis led the First Dryden Company of volunteers in the War of 1812. He acquired the liquor habit, as they used to say, although he later reformed and joined the church. While under the influence, according to reports, he would drill an imaginary battalion in the road outside his house, giving commands and carrying them out.

The Ellis Hollow Community Center was established in 1952, and it held the first Ellis Hollow Fair in 1953, an annual early September event in Tompkins County.

A Short History of Tompkins County

23. Mill at Enfield. The old grain mill (the east side is shown here) dating from 1838 was used as a park pavilion until the late 1970s.

Enfield

Located on the western border of the county in rolling country is the town of Enfield; its central waterway, Enfield (or Five Mile) Creek, forms one of the most beautiful gorges of the region (figure 1). In 1798 Jabez Hanner settled on the Ulysses-Enfield town line and was followed several years later in 1804 by Judah Baker and John Giltner, who moved into the forest. Giltner soon left, but Baker with his wife and seven children became the town's first permanent residents. At one time Baker owned most of the land now occupied by Enfield Center. In 1805 other groups came and settled near what is now Bostwick Corners (where the Wallenbeck Inn was built) and also at Applegate Corners, location of the first tavern in 1807 and the first school in 1809, as well as a store. Applegate Corners probably became the commercial center of the

Growth and Development: The Communities

24. Enfield Farm. This picture was taken around the turn of the century. Horses were used for plowing well into the twentieth century.

town because the Catskill Turnpike (sometimes called the Jericho Turnpike for its original terminus in Jericho, now Bainbridge) —which was chartered in 1804 and originally ran from Richford on the east, through Caroline, Dryden, and Ithaca—passed through Applegate Corners on its way west. The town's first sawmill was built in 1812 by Benjamin Ferris near the Enfield Falls, and 1817 saw the first gristmill in the same location. A later grain mill put up by Jared Treman about 1838 was used until recently as a pavilion in the state park at Enfield Glen (figure 23).

The town was created from the town of Ulysses in 1821 and received its name from Enfield in Connecticut. The small community had five church organizations between 1817 and 1844, as the population grew and occupied itself with settling the land (figure 24). Despite its small population, Enfield sent 100 men to fight in the Civil War. In the early years of the twentieth century Robert H. Treman of Ithaca acquired parcels of land at and around the glen and in 1920 turned the property over to the local park authorities. In 1923 it was deeded to the state and became part of the Fin-

25. Parking at Enfield Glen. The old grain mill is to the right.

ger Lakes Park Commission under the name of Robert H. Treman State Park (figure 25).

Groton

Located in the northeast corner of the county and in many ways oriented toward Cortland, the town of Groton started out with two main resources: good soil and waterpower from the Owasco Inlet and Fall Creek. Over the years it has been a manufacturing center—of cheese, in both Groton Village and McLean, iron and machinery, bridges, carriages, and typewriters. The community was first part of Locke. Major Benjamin Hicks of Canajoharie owned lot #75 in the town; it was settled by John Perrin from Massachusetts, who worked for Hicks. Perrin built a house and spent the winter of 1797/8 there. The first gristmill was put up in 1802, followed within a few years by a school and a church. The post office was established in 1812, with a boy on horseback bringing the mail once a week from Homer. In 1817 the town was formed from Locke (designated as #18 of the Military Tract) and was called Division; in 1818 it became Groton, named by its set-

Growth and Development: The Communities

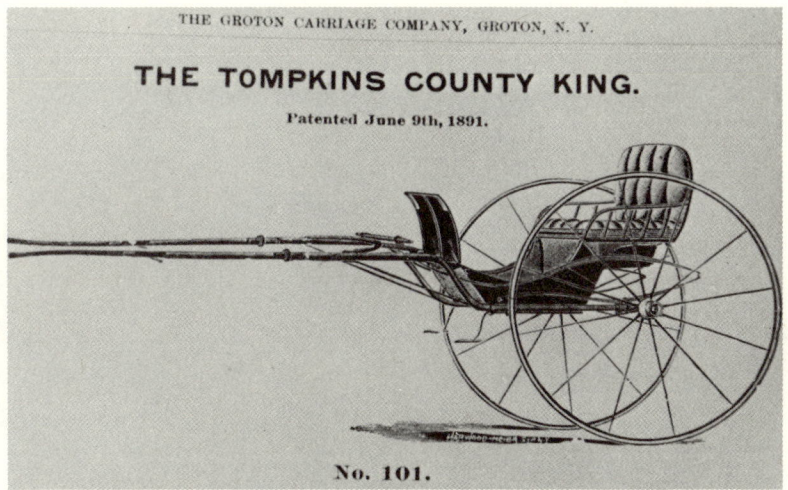

26. Groton Carriage. This vehicle is one of many different carriages manufactured by the Groton Carriage Company.

tlers for Groton, Massachusetts. The village of Groton was incorporated in 1860 and reincorporated in 1890.

The village, a station on the Southern Central Railroad, was the center of the town's manufacturing. The Groton Bridge & Manufacturing Company, an outgrowth of the Groton Iron Works (a foundry and machine shop that opened in 1849), began in 1877 to manufacture iron bridges; most of its buildings were destroyed by fire in 1961 (see figure 40). The Groton Carriage Company grew from a small carriage business in 1855 to a successful large enterprise that operated until about 1910 (figure 26). In 1909 began the manufacture in Groton of typewriters with interchangeable type, soon to be given the name Corona. Later the company was merged with the L. C. Smith Typewriter Company of Syracuse in 1925 and with W. Marchant Calculators in 1958, forming the Smith Corona Marchant Corporation. The Groton typewriter plant has only recently been shut down.

The town of Groton contains several small villages. Peruville, which was settled in 1805, had established fourteen churches between that year and 1870; it was also a station on the Southern Central Railroad. McLean on Fall Creek, a station on the Utica,

27. Elm Tree Inn. Located on Fall Creek Road in McLean, the inn is shown around 1900, when the elm tree was over one hundred years old. The wooden bridge in the foreground crosses Fall Creek.

Ithaca & Elmira Railroad, was originally called Moscow; the name was changed in 1824 to that of the first postmaster. It has its own post office today. The Elm Tree Inn stands on the site of a log tavern built there by early settler Amasa Cobb in 1796; in front stood an enormous elm tree, a cross-section of which is still displayed today (figure 27). Groton City, in the northeastern corner of the county, is also on Fall Creek and in early days had many sawmills; in those times it was known as Slab City.

West Groton, a farming community in the northwestern corner

Growth and Development: The Communities

28. West Groton Church. This drawing from a recent photograph was made for the Groton Historical Society.

of the town, has one of the oldest church buildings in the county. The Congregational Church on West Groton Road was organized in 1816 with five members; the building was put up in 1832, its steeple built in 1884 (figure 28).

Lansing

On April 17, 1817, the town of Lansing was created (under the act that created Tompkins County) from the lower half, military lots #41 to #100, of Milton (Military Township #17). It was named for John Lansing, a distinguished member of a prominent New York State family and state controller in charge of land grants at the time. The town has been involved in a variety of activities and businesses, from boat building to manufacturing of cement and mining of salt. Today, on the southern border of the town, are the county airport, four shopping malls, and the new YMCA.

A Short History of Tompkins County

Lansing was once the domain of the Cayuga Indians who had two settlements, one on Salmon Creek, the other at Esty's on the lakeshore. When the Indians were driven away by Sullivan's expedition, the land was left open for the white settlers. At the time the territory was so densely covered that the Indians called it Dark Forest and Esty's was called Forest City. The first white settlers were Silas and Henry Ludlow and Henry's son, Major Thomas Ludlow, who came by way of Athens on the Susquehanna. The men arrived at the head of the lake in February 1791 and went north on the ice until they reached the Salmon Creek outlet. They went up the ravine and found the falls, which would provide waterpower (figure 29). They purchased lot #76 for $60 and they built a sawmill of logs, twenty feet square, below the falls and the first gristmill. At about the same time several Pennsylvania Dutch families settled in the southern part of the town. In 1792 Andrew Myers came from Maryland and built a cabin at the mouth of the creek; his son also put up a sawmill and a gristmill. The Townley brothers, Richard and Charles, built a log cabin, which they occupied at Christmas 1792, near the present South Lansing Road. Pioneer Thomas North built a log cabin on lot #71, at the corner of Searles and Conlon roads, around 1800; in 1847 the cabin was removed log by log and rebuilt farther north. It is now on the grounds of the Cayuga Museum of History and Art in Auburn. Samuel Baker, the first supervisor of Milton, bought lot #54 and settled near Lake Ridge. Daniel Clark settled in 1803 in Ludlowville and became a dealer in potash, a product of the early forest clearing. He transported it to Albany and exchanged it for dyestuffs and articles for his family; this involved a round trip of six weeks through the mud.

Between 1796 and 1849 nine churches were established in the area, and for many years Ludlowville was the largest village in the town. Lansingville, first called Teetertown after settler Conrad Teeter, was a gathering with cabins and a tavern. There was also a large settlement at Libertyville, now South Lansing.

The township was originally called Milton; a portion was taken off in 1802 and added to Locke; the name was changed to Genoa in 1808. In its early days the town had eight distilleries; the Lansing

29. Ludlowville. The Salmon Creek Falls can be seen to the right of this panoramic view taken in 1907.

30. Rogues Harbor Inn at South Lansing. A brochure from the time of Colonel McIntyre in the early 1900s described it as the Rogues Harbor Country Club, "a home for automobiles and touring parties." The elms were planted by McIntyre as good-sized trees. (Photograph by Marion Wesp, courtesy of Lois O'Connor)

Town Temperance Society was founded on New Year's Eve, 1827. Between 1830 and 1836 the Central Exchange Hotel—so called because the stagecoach horses changed there—was built, at a cost of $40,000, by General Daniel D. Minier, son of early settler Abram Minier who had lived on the site in 1792. The hotel, a colonial structure of brick, originally had classical pillars and wrought-iron balconies around two sides and the front; it is still in operation today (figure 30). The story goes that it was christened the Rogues Harbor by a man who threw a whiskey bottle at it from across the street. An earlier account, however, indicates that the village at Libertyville was known already in 1822 as the "Rogue's Harbor."[6] Among the notables who stayed at the hotel were William Seward, governor of the state and Lincoln's secretary of state, and

Growth and Development: The Communities

31. Ludlowville Cornet Band (1895). The young man on the left in this photograph taken at Cayuga Lake Park is the band's mascot.

Tompkins County's most famous murderer, Edward Rulloff, who after teaching school in Dryden became a Lansing resident. For a while, when Lansing prohibited the sale of alcoholic beverages, the hotel was called the Cold Water Inn. North of Lansing was a half-mile racetrack, which was popular between 1840 and 1860.

Lansing played an important role in the railroad history of the county, in the New York, Auburn & Lansing Railroad, and especially as the terminus of the Short Line in the early twentieth century. The Cayuga Lake Railroad, chartered in 1867 and later part of the Lehigh Valley system, runs trains to this day which carry coal to the Milliken power station and return with salt from the Cayuga Rock Salt Company.

At one time the town had a cornet band with eighteen instruments (figure 31), and Lansing resident Eugene LaBarr played in John Philip Sousa's band, headed the New York City Police Band in 1938, and was in charge of music at the 1939 World's Fair. In 1962, twenty-four acres on the south side of the mouth of Salmon

Creek were set aside for a park and marina, with equipment and pavilions provided by the Lions Club.

Important industries have operated in Lansing along the lakeshore; in the 1830s, for example, there was canal boat building at Myers. The Penn-Dixie Company works at Portland Point at one time produced 2,000 barrels of high-grade cement a day. Its early kilns had wood fires. The Portland Cement Company works started in 1900 on the same site; in 1935 the works and buildings were swept away by flood but were quickly rebuilt; the company closed in June 1947. The quarry for the Cayuga Crushed Stone Company is located today at Portland Point. The first salt company was formed in 1887 (figure 84) and in 1921 the Cayuga Rock Salt Company was established. The New York State Electric & Gas Company's steam power plant at Milliken Station started generating in the fall of 1955. The village of Lansing was incorporated in 1974; it was established mainly to administer the commercial development of several large apartment complexes and the shopping malls.

Newfield

Located in the southwestern corner of the county, Newfield has a mainly hilly terrain and two waterways, the Cayuta Creek and the Cayuga Inlet Creek. The first settlers were Indians from the Tutelo and Catawba tribes. In a 1789 treaty the Indians surrendered their territory to the state, and the land south of the Military Tract was sectioned and parceled out in 1791. The purchaser was Thomas Livingston, and one-third of the Livingston Purchase was sold to Robert C. Johnson, a resident of Connecticut, who eventually sold his land, in the area called Saxton Hill, to his state. It was not until the middle of the nineteenth century that Connecticut ceased to be a landowner in the town, and today the hill, the highest elevation in the county at 2,097 feet, is still called Connecticut Hill. The first white settler, James Thomas, built near Poney Hollow in 1800. In the early days of the town there were several principal settlements; one was in Newfield Village where Eliaken Dean purchased the village site in 1802 and named the settlement Flor-

Growth and Development: The Communities

32. Newfield Village (c. 1890). This picture was developed and distributed by the Newfield Portrait Studio.

ence. He continued to reside in Ithaca but built the first sawmill and gristmill around 1810. Richard Seabring (or Sebring), who commanded a company in the Revolutionary army, moved to the area in 1804. His son Cornelius had been an early settler in Lansing, but he also moved to Newfield and became postmaster (the mail came once a week, carried on horseback between Ithaca, and Elmira) and town supervisor; their community was called the Seabring Settlement. There also were settlements at Trumbull's Corners (originally Rumsey's Corners) in the northern part of the town and at East Newfield, which was called Nina. The years between 1810 and 1815 saw an influx of settlers, mostly from the New York City area. Much later, around the turn of the century, another migration brought Finns and Czechs to live in Newfield.

33. Newfield in 1870. From left to right are the Goldsmith building, a cabinetmaker's house, the covered bridge, and the south end of the Old Newfield Hotel.

The town (see figure 32) was first organized as part of Tioga County in 1811, under the name Cayuta. In 1822 it was annexed to Tompkins County and got the name of Newfield—reportedly because of the abundance of ungranted land within its boundaries. Part of the town was annexed to what is now Schuyler County in 1853. A major fire burned out the center of the village in 1875, destroying all its records. The village (figure 33) was incorporated in 1895 but dissolved its charter in 1925. It remains unincorporated to this day. One of the county's landmarks is the Newfield Covered Bridge (figure 41).

Over the years the town has known more than its share of disasters—floods, fires, and blizzards. In the flood of 1905, seven bridges were out, and the 10 A.M. milk train was stranded near Stratton's Crossing for a week. The flood of 1935 washed out the bridges again, as well as some mills. During the blizzards in 1944/5 some roads were closed for a month, and in February 1958 food was dropped by helicopter to people on the Seeley and Connecticut hills, as it was in parts of Dryden as well.

Early on the village had a cloth-manufacturing and wool-carding factory and an industry in potash, which was used for fertilizer and for lye, and thus making soap. There was considerable business in lumber and in the export of deer skins and 1830 marked the start of a flour-mill business called the Newfield Flouring Mills, which used water and later stream power. In 1836 the town had five gristmills, of which two were within the village, and twenty-one sawmills. Even with all this activity the village in 1831 was still offering a $10 bounty on full-grown wolf skins.

Aside from the principal flour mills, which in the mid-1850s were both owned and run by P. S. Dudley and ground over 70,000 bushels of flour per year, Newfield's main industry until the past few years was its school system. The town's first schoolhouse was a log cabin near Bank Street in 1805, which was replaced by the Old Yellow School House. By 1822 there were twelve schoolhouses, and by 1870 twenty-one, most of which accommodated grades 1–6 or 1–8 in a single room. The school year was sometimes as short as three months. Only by the end of the century was high school education available. The central school district was formed in 1939 and became Newfield's largest employer. Today it has been surpassed as the town's biggest business by Brown Cow Farm, makers of yogurt. Most of the population now commutes to work in the Ithaca area, though some residents have remained on the land as farmers.

Ulysses

And last in line is the town that still holds the original name assigned to much of Tompkins County at the beginning of its history. Located on the west shore of Cayuga Lake, Ulysses has three principal waterways, Trumansburg and Willow creeks as well as

Taughannock Creek with its magnificent gorge and the highest perpendicular waterfall in the state (see figure 71). The earliest settlers here too were the Indians, whose villages on Taughannock Creek and near Waterburg escaped the raid by Colonel Dearborn and his men. These settlements were discovered by the early explorers from Kingston, some of whom eventually settled in Ithaca. Three of this group returned to what is now the town of Ulysses, however, and Samuel Weyburn built a cabin at Goodwin's Point, a spot on the Indian trail that skirted the lake (there was no other path at the time) which soon became a stopping place for travelers. Abner Treman (or Truman or a number of other possible spellings), who as a Revolutionary War veteran got 640 acres, drew lot #2, the area now occupied by the village of Trumansburg. His brother and son, walking from near Albany, arrived in June 1792 to settle the land, and Abner came by way of Chenango County in 1793. It is said that he drove his oxen down on to the flats during the winter of 1793/4 and let them browse. On his way back he stopped at Nathaniel Davenport's (a tavern on West Hill called the Old Stone Heap—still standing today; see figure 85), then walked to Weyburn's through a snow storm so severe that his feet were frozen. As a result he had a wooden leg the rest of his life, but it did not seem to curb his activities in any way. He built a tub gristmill in 1794, cleared the land, and sold lots from his parcel. The community that sprang up was called Treman's Village. When the post office opened in 1811, the name was altered to Trumansburg, although for years it was popularly known as Shin Hollow or The Hollar because, it is said, so many drunken men banged their shins when reeling home from the tavern.

The first tavern in the village was built by James McLallen, whose sister was the wife of Abner Treman. McLallen was also a merchant (he had a store built of brick on Main Street) and a farmer. His son D. K. (for David King) built a farm on Perry City Road, dating from 1848, and his descendants, the Robert McLallens, still live on the farm. Another early settler was eighteen-year-old Hermon Camp, who came on foot from Owego in 1805 to set up a general store. When the Tompkins County Bank opened its doors in 1836, he became its president, a post he held until 1859. He was also the first president of the Trumansburg Academy. In

Growth and Development: The Communities

34. Hermon Camp Mansion, Trumansburg.

1845 work was started on a Greek Revival house on Lawn (later Camp) Street (figure 34), which was completed in 1848 and made principally of local materials; in it Camp gave memorable parties and from its roof his youngest daughter, Hermione, flew a flag during the Civil War whenever there was a Union victory.

Another settlement at Jacksonville, once called Harlow's Corners, had religious organizations and a school by 1803. A third settlement was at Willow Creek. At Podunk a log meeting house was built in 1811 by the Presbyterians and later a Baptist church was organized there. Ulysses Township was originally divided among several different counties, but it became part of Tompkins when the county was organized in 1817. In 1821 Ithaca and Enfield were set off from the original township, and the present boundaries were fixed. The main settlement grew and prospered with stores, churches, and schools. The Ulysses Philomathic Library was es-

35. Trumansburg in 1935. The great July flood washed out most of the village center, and the A & P Market collapsed into the creek. In the center of the picture is the traffic signal in the middle of the street.

tablished in 1811. The community, however, was considered ungodly by many, because of the alarming proportions of drunkenness attained there. A town meeting was called in 1828 to deal with the problem; the temperance movement thus had an early start and was to prove a significant force in the village throughout the century.

Trumansburg Creek, running through the middle of the settlement, was spanned by a steep wooden bridge. Through the years parts of the village were flooded almost every time it rained heavily (figure 35)—a problem often described but without any solution having been found; upon several occasions (especially in 1833, 1905, and 1935), the dams, mills, factories, and bridges have been washed away. In the flood of 1935 the mill at Halseyville was swept over Taughannock Falls. A covered bridge was built around

36. Covered Bridge at Halseyville. The bridge, built by Dr. Lewis Halsey, is shown around 1908, complete with advertising.

1832 across Taughannock Creek at Halseyville, which was in use until 1927 (figure 36).

In the town were important stops on many transportation routes—the Ithaca & Geneva Turnpike, which opened in 1811, the Geneva, Ithaca & Sayre Railroad in the 1870s (in the early days the trip between Trumansburg and Ithaca took 2 hours and 17 minutes), and the lake boats and steamers, which stopped at Taughannock Point to pick up and discharge cargo and passengers.

The 1870s saw the start of a period of great prosperity and building for the village. The Opera Block went up in 1871, with stores on the first floor, offices on the second, and the opera house on the third (figure 37). There were several large hotels, the Phoenix House (James McLallen's home, originally built in 1835) and the Trembley House; at the top of Taughannock Falls were two more large hotels, the Taughannock House (which on one weekend in

A Short History of Tompkins County

37. Opera Block, Main Street in Trumansburg (c. 1900).

August of 1875 served 1,500 dinners) and the Cataract House (which served 962 meals during the Fourth of July weekend of the same year). During the 1880s the lake boats had great popularity and Trumansburg Landing, where the *Frontenac* (figures 73 and 74) docked, became something of a summer resort. One of the county's most important industries got started in 1890 when the Morse brothers began to manufacture carts with a special spring mechanism in Trumansburg. In 1922 the entire Opera Block burned, as did the school in 1924. The new state park of 64 acres at Taughannock opened the summer of 1925.

Trumansburg today has its share of farms as well as small businesses, the most prominent being housed in an old block on Main Street that backs on the creek. Among them are the MacDonald's Farm Market, the Rongovian Embassy restaurant, and one of the area's independent publishing houses, The Crossing Press. The village was incorporated in 1872, and today is an important community in the county, well known as a lively artistic center.

[3]

Transportation and Communication

ACCUSTOMED as we are to the Tompkins County of today—with modern roads, paved streets, motorized vehicles, an expanding airport, and electronic telecommunications—it is hard to imagine the transportation picture of the past. The changes over the years—from single-file trails to four-lane highways, from wagon and coach to airplane, from word-of-mouth to automatic-dial telephone—are enormous and complex (figure 38). Indeed the transportation story is central in our history, a key factor in the extent of the county's commercial development. Back in the first half of the nineteenth century, the view was widely held that our region would become a great center for commerce in the developing country, an important link in the movement of goods and people from one part of the United States to another.

The prediction was not realized, for various reasons, and our region has remained, in the words of one wit, "centrally isolated." Today the airport serves as a connector only; we do not have many links to major cities. The principal east-west highways of the state, the Thruway to the north and Route 17 to the south, both pass by us at a considerable distance. The nearest major north-south route, Interstate 81, runs about thirty miles east of us. We no longer have a passenger train, and bus service is limited. Ithaca and its surroundings have maintained a fairly constant population over the years (the large increases have come only in the past three decades), partly because of terrain (no railroad completely solved the prob-

38. State and Cayuga Streets in Ithaca. This view from around 1890 shows a scene very different from today's, with the street trolley and snow as essential for transportation. In the background is the Clinton House in Second Empire style, complete with square cupola and mansard roof. Behind can be seen the spire of St. John's Episcopal Church (built in 1860) and the tower of the old Ithaca High School building (figure 58).

lems of the hills, nor have the highway engineers either), partly because of national and regional financial crises, partly because of weather and resources. Many residents of the county count this isolation as a blessing.

Roads and Bridges

The first routes of the area were Indian trails, mere footpaths that zigzagged through the dense woodland. Indian trails determined the way the two military groups from Sullivan's army followed on their mission of destruction. The early pioneers also used these trails to get to their land and to move between settlements, and many of our major roadways today still follow these primitive paths. These earliest routes were suited for travel on foot; most were not even wide enough for a rider on horseback. The first large group of pioneers to settle in our region came up an Indian trail from Owego, and they had to cut a way through for their wagons and carts. The Bridle Road crossing Dryden Village from Virgil to Ithaca was in many places so narrow that it could be traveled only on foot. When Hermon Camp came up the lake trail from Ithaca to the village of Trumansburg as late as 1805, he reported that "there was no real road, the smaller trees only were cut, and the road was very crooked or zigzag to avoid the larger trees."[7]

The Bridle Road marked the way for the present Route 13, just as Route 96 to the south was laid on the old trail from Owego used by the first settlers. The only early road between the east and west sides of the valley at the head of the lake was called Five Mile Drive, and it crossed Six Mile Creek at Aurora Street. A public road from Oxford on the Chenango River direct to Ithaca was built in 1791, and it became a major highway for migrants as well as part of the Catskill Turnpike.

Much of the gradual widening of these simple paths into roadways was done by the settlers themselves, who also built simple bridges over the streams (the bridges over the deeply cut gorges would not come until much later). Stumps and roots tripped up man and horse, and the spring rains turned the deeply rutted earth to paths of mud. Many farmers waited until winter to move their wheat because, once there was snow on the ground, transport by horse-drawn sleigh was relatively easy and fast.

The very early construction of the main roads was in private hands, often under state charter, and the first major public highways were owned by private companies and operated as turnpikes. Between 1797 and 1807 there were 88 companies, which had constructed over nine hundred miles of roads. With the War of 1812 public enthusiasm for toll roads mounted, and by 1821 the number of turnpike and bridge companies receiving state charters had grown to 278 with over four thousand miles built. Then interest in

[89]

39. Speed Tavern. This home in West Slaterville was a popular stagecoach stop on the Catskill Turnpike.

toll roads slowly waned as many of their functions were taken over by the canals and railroads. By 1840 most of the turnpikes had proved unprofitable and were taken over by the state.

Every ten miles or so along the turnpike was a tollhouse, and a barrier somewhat like a fence of logs which swung across the entire road. The gate was turned upon payment of the toll. Along these roads traveled wagons, stagecoaches, herds of cattle and sheep, itinerant pedlars, and farm vehicles—as well as much of the mail. Teamsters walked beside wagons loaded with wheat, flour, potash, and other local products, mainly agricultural; most aimed to make twenty miles per day. Taverns for the wagoners and stagecoach passengers sprang up along the roadside, and the innkeeper was an important person in those days (figure 39). Stagecoaches provided most of the public transportation until the railroads took over in the 1830s, and many stagecoach routes are used by the buses today.

Transportation and Communication

The major turnpikes of our region were built in the early years of the nineteenth century. In 1811 both the Ithaca & Owego and Ithaca & Geneva turnpikes were opened; the former operated for forty-one years. The best-known and most widely traveled of these roads, however, was the Catskill Turnpike, also called the Bath & Jericho Turnpike and chartered in 1804. Originally the eastern terminus was in Richford, and the highway crossed Tompkins County, generally on the line of Route 79, on west to Bath near the head of Seneca Lake. The road was then extended to the east, to Jericho (now Bainbridge), and later all the way to Catskill on the Hudson, thus making a vital connection via the river boats to New York City and points south. The stagecoach made stops at the Ithaca Hotel (see figure 8), the Tompkins House, and the Clinton House after it opened in 1830 (figures 38 and 87). In 1835 the mail coach left every evening at 8 and, with lodging at Delhi that night, arrived in Catskill in time for the 5 P.M. boats from Albany and New York. The journey of 160 miles cost $6. The first tollgate east of Ithaca was located near the present intersection of Route 79 and Pine Tree Road and was built of logs.

Over the years trails gave way to roads and the quality of the roads improved, but still travelers had to contend with dust in the summer and frozen ruts and snow drifts in the winter, not to mention the mud brought by the spring rains. The middle of the nineteenth century brought an apparent solution, a boom in the building of wooden plank roads, especially upstate since ample lumber was available. Unfortunately such roads did not wear well and soon proved dangerous. Like the turnpikes that preceded them, the plank roads seldom earned enough revenue to pay for repairs. The roads we know today did not really start to come into existence until the 1920s. Many of the big bridges came only with the modernization of the roadways; the viaduct over Salmon Creek in Lansing, for example, was built in 1929/30. The rebuilding of Route 13 to the southwest, with the Newfield bypass, was completed in 1960, whereas the improved four-lane road in the other direction was not finished until the mid-1960s.

The problem of getting across the waterways and gorges, especially in the Ithaca area, was solved slowly. Very early wooden bridges were built across the creeks, but the first iron bridge, over

40. Stewart Avenue Bridge. This deck truss span over Cascadilla Creek built in 1889 is one of several county bridges constructed by the Groton Bridge Company, which also made steel frames for buildings in the area.

Six Mile Creek at Aurora Street, was not erected until 1870. After David B. Stewart took office as the first mayor of the newly chartered city of Ithaca, the city extended Factory Street (later Stewart Avenue) in about 1890 with an iron bridge over the Cascadilla Creek gorge (figure 40); not only did this open a tract of land for development, it gave Cornell students a way of getting to the campus other than across the gorge at the bottom of the hill and up through the cemetery. In 1896 one of Cornell's benefactors, William H. Sage, gave money to replace a wooden bridge (at College Avenue) at the south entrance of the campus with a stone arch. In the following year the present Triphammer Bridge was built (previously Fall Creek had acted as the city's northern boundary), providing a way to the Heights. Before only a footbridge at the bottom of the Beebe Lake Dam had provided this link. The Stewart Avenue Bridge over Fall Creek gorge was constructed in 1900, completing the trolley loop, and in 1901 Edward G. Wyckoff, who owned much of Cornell Heights as well as the trolley line, granted permission to the university to build and maintain a footbridge across Fall Creek. It was replaced by a suspension bridge in 1904.

The most celebrated bridge of the county is not in Ithaca, however; it is the covered bridge in Newfield spanning the Cayuga Inlet Creek (figure 41). Built as part of the old plank road to Ithaca, it is the sole survivor of three covered bridges in Tompkins County (see figures 17 and 36). Built on the site of a log bridge dating from 1812, when the hamlet was called Florence, the covered span, 115 feet long and 16 feet wide, was put up between 1851 and 1853. Labor and lumber were cheap then—the total cost amounted to only $800. Originally the bridge had a solid siding for its entire length; later, diamond-shaped openings were cut to admit light. It is said that $200 was donated to pay an artist to decorate the bridge with a mural similar to those in the wooden bridges of Lucerne in Switzerland, but the artist died, and then the Civil War put a stop to such plans. The oldest covered bridge in daily use in New York State, it is one of twenty-five such structures remaining. The bridge was completely restored in 1972.

Waterways

The region's creeks have been used principally for waterpower over the years and only rarely for the transportation of people and goods. The lake, however, has been an essential waterway from the beginning of the county's history. With the entire length of the Erie Canal completed in 1825, and with the Cayuga & Seneca Canal opened from Cayuga Village to Montezuma on the Erie Canal in 1828, Tompkins County was integrated into a very large trans-

41. Newfield Bridge. Inside the covered bridge can be seen evidence of its special construction: uninterrupted crisscross diagonals, called the Town lattice truss pattern.

portation network. At that time plans called for a canal between the Susquehanna River and the head of Cayuga Lake, but the project was quickly abandoned. With the chartering of the Ithaca & Owego Railroad the idea grew for a second canal between the headwaters of Cayuga Lake (the boat landing where Cascadilla Creek met Cayuga Street in Ithaca) via part of the Erie Canal to Sodus Bay on Lake Ontario. Deep-water ships would convey raw materials from the Middle West through the Great Lakes via this Sodus Bay Canal to Ithaca; here mills would convert these materials into finished goods, which would then be moved out to markets to the south, east, and west. Coal from the rich Pennsylvania fields and lumber, grain, shingles, and plaster would move in and through and out of the region.

With the completion of the railroad between Ithaca and Owego, part of this great commercial dream came true: Ithaca did become a distribution point for the coal of Pennsylvania. But the Sodus Bay Canal was never built. Though later in the century the railroads would capture most of the lake and canal business, for several decades Cayuga Lake was a busy transportation artery.

Samuel Baker, one of Lansing's earliest settlers, built the first canal boat to run from Cayuga Lake, and canal boat building was an important industry on the east shore of the lake and along the Inlet throughout the nineteenth century. The Cayuga Steamboat Company was organized in 1819 and the steamboat *Enterprise*, built on the bank of the Cayuga Inlet, made its trial trip on June 1, 1820. A steamboat landing site was soon built at Port Renwick at the southeast corner of the lake (figures 44, 69, and 74), as the Inlet was obstructed by a sandbar. Later in the century steamboats would have a landing at the meeting of the Inlet and Cascadilla Creek (figure 73). By 1829 steamboats were moving up and down the lake; the *Telemachus* and later the *DeWitt Clinton* went between Ithaca and Cayuga Village, making the round trip in a day (the fare was $1, with meals extra). These and other boats met with stagecoaches that went directly to Catskill and Newburgh on the Hudson, thus making connections with New York City and New Jersey. Travelers could go from Newburgh to Buffalo in three days—two days on the stage from Newburgh to Ithaca, an overnight on the lake, and then from Cayuga Village to Buffalo in a day. Apparently business was good, as reports of the time say the boats were very crowded. And during the 1850s and 1860s canal boats moved goods up the Hudson, across the Erie Canal, through the Montezuma link, and south on Cayuga Lake. These goods were then carted around the region. Return boats took local agricultural products back to markets in the east.

Railroads

The story of the railroads in Tompkins County is a complicated one, and nowhere is the crucial role of our special terrain more apparent. During the nineteenth century railroad schemes of a dizzying variety were thought up. Many of these projects received charters, many attracted financial backing, but only a very few were ultimately realized. The essential problem was always the "Ithaca link": the route to connect the different railroad lines coming to the county seat from various sides had to solve the riddle of Ithaca's hills. A solution of sorts was reached, but it was not a particularly good one, and in the end the railroads (or at least those providing passenger service) were dropped as a commercial venture.

Until 1850 all railroad companies were granted charters by private acts of the New York State Legislature, which provided that construction should begin within three years and railroad operation within six, with a toll of 3 cents a mile per passenger. With this arrangement, many companies received charters for their planned routes; very few railroads, however, got beyond the planning stages.

With the completion of the Erie Canal and Ithaca's access to it through Cayuga Lake, local capitalists saw potential revenue in freight payments, storage, and shipping charges, and they dreamed of Ithaca as an important place in a massive interchange of goods. There was a missing link in this scheme, however, between the Susquehanna River and Ithaca. A railroad was supposed to provide that link, and the Ithaca & Owego Railroad was chartered in 1828. (Another project envisioned a railroad to the Hudson River, and the Catskill & Ithaca Railroad was chartered the same year; it was never built.)

A survey for the I&O was finished early in 1828, and the route along Six Mile Creek, with its rise over South Hill, was chosen. From the Inlet the route extended in a semicircle to the foot of the hill, just below the site of the old Morse Chain plant. From there an inclined plane rose sharply; trains were to be pulled up horses to the level road bed at the top. Bids for grading and materials were tendered in 1831, but building was slow. Despite legal difficulties and practical problems, however, two miles were completed in July 1833—a gala celebration was held and about one thousand people got free rides in both directions. The official opening did not take place until April 2, 1834, when a train pulled by horses and consisting of 49 cars, of which all but four (for passengers) carried plaster and salt, made the trip to Owego from the top of the hill at Ithaca. One eyewitness report in the *Ithaca Chronicle* described the road as a "succession of beautiful curves" and told readers that the cars got to Owego (a distance of twenty-nine miles) in three hours, exclusive of stops.[8] When the line was finally completed, the trip was made in less time, but the original idea of running trains through the winter months proved impracticable, and the maintenance of the track very costly. The company had to borrow from the state within five years, but at least the railroad was in existence.

The Ithaca & Owego was the second railroad chartered in the state and the fourth to open to the public. It turned out to be a proving ground for the principles of basic railroading. There were no signals, nor any fixed schedules. When two trains met on the single track, the cars of one train would have to be taken off the track. Freight trains had priority over passenger trains, so the cars of the latter would be removed "with the aid of horses and passengers" and then replaced once the freight train had passed.[9] The type of track used was something of an experiment, and an unsatisfactory one; two years after the line had opened, much of the road was out of repair. The introduction of the steam locomotive (the first engines burned wood) did not improve matters, although on a good run the journey could now be made in ninety minutes. Lack of patronage, inefficient operation (due mainly to sheer lack of experience), and the nationwide financial panic of 1837 brought the Ithaca & Owego serious problems. It was auctioned off in May 1842, the stock bought by a successor company called the Cayuga & Susquehanna Railroad.

A new route out of Ithaca, by Buttermilk Creek, was adopted, and an act of legislature required a rebuilding with modern rail. Then controlling interest in the company passed to financiers from outside the region, except for Josiah B. Williams (who had been involved in other Tompkins County financial projects, including the building of the Clinton House), and reconstruction began in 1849. The new route started at the steamboat landing, ran up the Inlet Valley to Buttermilk Creek, then swung around on a gravel-filled trestle and started up the hill. A switchback was built on South Hill to avoid the expense of bridging the ravines near Six Mile Creek, and the route joined the old railbed about four miles south. But for this switchback (which worked but caused delays), the route would probably have become the through route for the area. In 1851 a connection was made between the southern end of the line and a Pennsylvania railroad, and the first load of coal came north in 24 cars. With new track, abundant freight, and no competition, the railroad made a profit. It was linked in 1855 with the Delaware, Lackawanna & Western, which later bought it out.

With the success of the C&S came proposals to extend the line to the north. But the problem of linking lines from the northeast and east with those from the south and southwest was never completely solved. Even after the Civil War Ithaca was still served by the one railroad, its schedules slowed by the switchback arrangement; in addition connections to the New York Central via lake barges were subject in the winter to bad weather and inevitable interruptions.

The 1870s ushered in an era of prosperity and renewed interest in railroad building. The year 1871 saw eight different companies involved in active construction. Ezra Cornell, seeing the need for improved railroad service, proposed a link along Cascadilla Creek from East Hill to a junction with the Ithaca & Athens Railroad that opened for business in August 1871. This line had opened the fast route to the south, with track along the Inlet Creek and out east of Newfield Hill. One train ran daily in either direction, with stops at Nina (East Newfield), Stratton's, and West Danby; it then crossed Tioga County to Athens (just south of Sayre in Pennsylvania), a journey of three hours. In May of the same year the Ithaca & Cortland Railroad had started conveying passengers to the Ithaca town line, and in October it merged with another company to form the Utica, Ithaca & Elmira Railroad. The line from Cortland was extended over Cascadilla Creek and a small shanty was built on the grounds of Cornell University (near the present Bard Hall), which served as a depot. Trains had to back into or out of the terminus until the East Ithaca Depot on Maple Avenue opened in 1876. The idea of building through Ithaca was eventually abandoned, despite detailed plans for a cog railway along Cascadilla Creek (a locomotive with a cog on the front axle was actually delivered in 1875 but, judged of no use, was sent back).

In 1872 more progress was made on the different systems. The

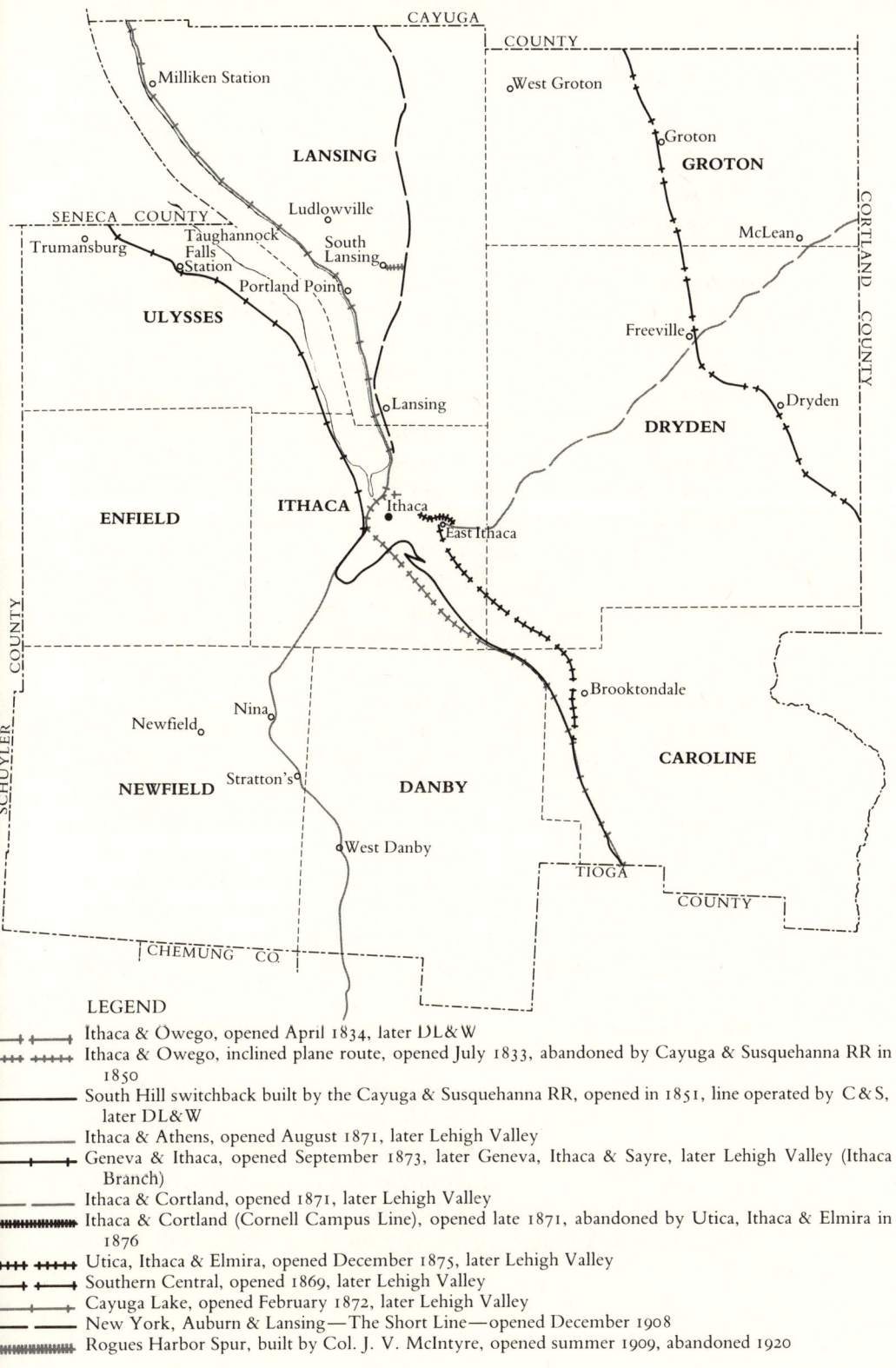

Map 3. Railroads in Tompkins County

Utica, Ithaca & Elmira extended its route more to the south, and from East Hill the line provided sporadic transportation to Freeville and Cortland. At Freeville travelers could change trains for the Southern Central to Auburn or for the Midland to Scipio Center (see figure 21). The Ithaca & Athens Railroad also improved its service to Philadelphia, but the important event of the year was when the Cayuga Lake Railroad with track between Ithaca and Cayuga Village, ran its first train from Athens to Cayuga, thus making the long-desired connection between the south and the New York Central. A special excursion train ran over the combined lines of the Ithaca & Athens and the Cayuga Lake railroads; it left Philadelphia at 8:30 A.M. for Ithaca, then proceeded to Cayuga, and on to Rochester and Niagara Falls. There the party spent the following day and returned over the same route, stopping at every station along the lake for speeches and celebrations and a cornet band concert at Ludlowville. Excursions ran during the summer, particularly to Atwaters, a private resort on the east shore of the lake, just north of the county line; Taughannock Landing, north of Lansing, was also a stop, and there a steamboat took visitors to see the falls on the west side of the lake.

In 1873 came national financial panic, which eventually bankrupted several of the county's railroads. Despite the crisis, however, the Utica, Ithaca & Elmira completed its line in 1875 from East Ithaca to Van Ettenville and then to Horseheads, with the railroad crossing Six Mile Creek on a timber trestle (figure 42). Lines between Geneva and Ithaca and on to the south had been consolidated in 1874, and the resulting Geneva, Ithaca & Sayre after several transformations became a Lehigh Valley subsidiary in 1890 (later known as the Lehigh Valley-Ithaca Branch). The main line of the Lehigh Valley bypassed Ithaca altogether because of the grade. The Cayuga Lake line was sold to the Geneva, Ithaca & Sayre and thus was incorporated into the Lehigh system as well, and by 1905 every branch railroad except the DL&W was part of the Lehigh system. When Ezra Cornell died in 1874, it was said that he had invested $2 million of his fortune in the local railroads.

The last railroad to be built in the county was chartered in 1900 as the New York, Auburn & Lansing. Of an entire transit system designed to link nearby cities, only the line between Auburn and

Transportation and Communication

42. Utica, Ithaca & Elmira Railroad. The wooden trestle bridge over Six Mile Creek at Brooktondale was completed in 1875 and replaced with a steel structure in 1894. See also figure 15.

Ithaca was completed. Constructed with 29 miles of steam road between Auburn and South Lansing and 7 miles of electric line from South Lansing to Ithaca, the southern section was done late in 1908, and on January 1, 1909, passenger service was inaugurated. This, the Short Line, became an interest of the Ithaca trolley company; the cars for the electric segment were leased from the Ithaca Street Railway. Train and city used the same power source, and so whenever a heavy load was being hauled, the lights would dim throughout Ithaca. The use of the trolley tracks from the Renwick station (where Stewart Park is today) into the city created a connection with the public transit system and the downtown. In 1909 a branch was built to run from the South Lansing depot to

Rogues Harbor, and for a time it made six trips a day. Slowly the service was reduced, however, until it was discontinued in 1920; the Short Line ceased operation three years later.

Well into the twentieth century Tompkins County had good passenger service, with three daily trains to Owego on the DL&W and connections to New York. The line was heavily used by students, who were often offered specials, but the unavoidable delays of the switchback connection proved tiresome. The Lehigh Valley-Ithaca Branch, on the other hand, provided an uninterrupted, often elegant ride to New York City in one direction and to Buffalo in the other. In those days one could ride the famous Black Diamond, a luxurious train that offered sleeping car accommodations and modern comfort. Cars for Philadelphia were switched onto the Reading Railroad at Bethlehem. Cornell University came to rely on the Lehigh Valley Railroad, which offered all sorts of specials: for parents, for vacationing students, for football games (especially to Philadelphia for the Penn game). In the 1930s the Auburn and Ithaca branch, which ran along the lakeside, ran observation trains for people to watch the crew races in the spring. Locomotives were attached at each end to a train with eight to fifteen cars, which operated on a push/pull system (figure 43). In 1939 the Lehigh Valley even painted its locomotives red, and the coaches featured Cornell Red decor.

Rail service was nonetheless dwindling as people found they could travel more conveniently in cars, more rapidly in planes, more cheaply in buses. Trucks took more and more of the freight business, and one by one the trains were taken off. In 1942 the DL&W discontinued passenger service, though it carried freight until 1956. The Lehigh Valley was allowed to abandon its passenger trains in 1959, much to the dismay of local residents. On May 11 of that year the Black Diamond made its final trip, and in August 1961 the last freight train ran between Ithaca and Trumansburg. In the 1970s and 1980s some rail service lingered on, but gradually the trains—with the exception of the 21-mile stretch of the Van Etten-Ithaca branch including the 14-mile line between Ithaca and Lake Ridge—ceased operations. The trains today make one round trip daily, carrying coal from Pennsylvania to NYSE&G's Milliken Station and returning with salt from the Ca-

43. Observation Train. The crowds really came out to watch the crew races along the eastern shore of Cayuga Lake. One of the train's two locomotives can be seen in the background.

yuga Salt Company mines to be shipped as far south as Baltimore. The Lehigh Valley became part first of the Penn Central system and then, in 1975, ConRail. Freight trains still rumble through downtown Ithaca twice a day, blocking traffic—interminably, it seems—to and from West Hill. But as we sit in our cars and wait (and continue to wait) at the railroad crossing, we can think back to the Black Diamond, to all those excursion trains, to all those specials. And, if we're in the right spot, we can look at the shiny old train attached to what was once the Lehigh Valley station, both beautifully restored and put to good use as a restaurant.

A Short History of Tompkins County
Public Transportation

The first public transportation in the county was the stagecoach, and from the early years passengers were offered frequent service into and out of Ithaca. With the link by lake to the Erie Canal, the combination of coach plus steamboat offered a variety of extended routes. Many of these old stagecoach routes were eventually taken over by the bus companies, and the Greyhound to New York City, for example, traverses part of the old Catskill Turnpike. Travel was slow in the early days; the route to Catskill, 160 miles distant, usually took two days. Traffic could be heavy; at times two four-horse carriages were hooked together, with a baggage wagon trailing behind. Taverns along the road offered refreshment and sometimes lodging to the travelers and places to change horses.

Buses and airplanes now provide these same transportation services. Several airlines fly from Tompkins County Airport, and the Greyhound now serves the Syracuse airport, making connections with major air service there. Part of US Air, one of the country's largest carriers, had its origins in a small private company started in Ithaca. A pilot named C. S. Robinson in 1945 often flew a private plane from Ithaca to the New York area; so frequently did businessmen and university executives and professors hitch rides on the plane that he inaugurated passenger service. In 1947, the first year of operations for Robinson, the airline carried 21,000 passengers (figure 46). In 1952 it became Mohawk Airlines, which moved to headquarters in Oneida in 1957. Mohawk was taken over by Allegheny Airlines, which eventually became part of US Air.

Public transportation inside Ithaca came by way of a horse-car line that ran from the Ithaca Hotel to the Geneva, Ithaca & Sayre (later Lehigh Valley) Railroad station and to the steamboat landing. A trolley system, introduced in 1884/5 under the name of the Ithaca Street Railway Company, first ran a line in 1887/8 (not a regular service) on State Street from the Ithaca Hotel to the railroad station. In 1891 Herman Bergholtz and Horace E. Hand bought the trolley and electric companies; they built a waterwheel plant in the Fall Creek gorge, which generated hydroelectric power for the trolleys until it burned in 1905. The trolley company in May 1892 got a franchise to operate a line on Tioga Street along with the line on State Street, and a year later trolley service opened between the East Ithaca station on Maple Avenue and the downtown Ithaca station of the Elmira & Cortland Branch-Auburn Division. The company ran a single track up East Hill, and the first car made the climb in January 1893. The railway entered the Cornell campus over a bridge, built the same year. A spur was then added, and cars ran across the campus along South and East avenues for fifteen years until the spur west of East Avenue was torn up in 1910. In the early 1900s the trolleys also climbed South Hill.

Herman Bergholtz, engineer of the street railway, became associated with developer Edward G. Wyckoff, who owned much of Cornell Heights. Together they formed the Ithaca Heights Land Company, with the purpose of developing the street railway and opening up Cornell Heights to development. In 1899, with aid from Wyckoff, the railway extended its line along Thurston Avenue and in 1900, with the completion of the bridge across Fall Creek just below the power plant, continued around to Stewart Avenue and then to University Avenue, making a car line loop. The first cars circled the loop in 1900, and for quite a while this route proved very popular, offering a splendid view of the lake where the tracks rounded the hill at Inspiration Point (now The Knoll).

The electric transit system allowed the city to spread out. The old north branch of Six Mile Creek was filled in, and the area between Titus Avenue and Clinton Street became available for home sites. In 1894 the Cayuga Lake Railroad Company purchased lakeshore property from the Renwick estate and ran a line from Railroad Avenue to the lake; forty acres were developed at the terminus as Renwick (later Stewart) Park. The trolley lines up East Hill and to the north of the Fall Creek gorge opened up the land in Cornell Heights. A track was built from the car line at Thurston Avenue on Highland and Wyckoff avenues and Kline Road and then northwest to Renwick. For a year the service was very popular, but then business dwindled, and the tracks were torn up. In 1905 another loop was built still farther north, curving back by the lake with a terminus in Renwick Park (figure 44). The extension on the Heights line led to the rapid development of Cayuga

44. Ithaca Street Railway (1906). The Heights trolley line extension provided its passengers with quite a view. The steamboat pier and Renwick Park buildings are clearly visible in the background.

Heights. The street railway also played its part in the Short Line between Ithaca and Auburn, as it leased the cars for the electric-powered Ithaca-Lansing segment of the journey.

Little by little, however, the trolley service lost popularity; it was finally ended in 1930. Bus service eventually replaced it, but considerable time elapsed before the city of Ithaca got a good public transportation network. Today Ithaca Transit runs six different hourly bus routes, which begin in front of the Woolworth store on East Green Street and serve all four corners of the city and some areas beyond. In addition, the Northeast Transit Bus, operated by Swarthout & Ferris, provides service from Ithaca to Cayuga Heights, the Northeast, and Lansing. Also the East Ithaca Transit and the Caravan, which goes from Ithaca to Brooktondale and Slaterville Springs, run on a regular schedule. A Chemung County bus provides transport service between Watkins Glen and the Cornell campus. Gadabout offers special bus service for the elderly, and Cornell University runs its own buses to and from various sides of the campus. The most rapidly developing transportation line is TomTran, under the direction of the Tompkins County Planning Board, which offers service from the Ithaca Commons several times a day to communities all over the county: Dryden, Etna, Freeville, Groton Village, Pyramid Mall in Lansing, Newfield, and Trumansburg.

Postal Service—Telephone—Telegraph

From their first settlement most small communities in the county had their own post offices, the postmaster being appointed by local government. At the beginning men or boys carried mail on foot or on horseback and distributed it to the community post offices about once a week. Very often the post office was in the postmaster's or another resident's home or in the general store. One post office in the town of Caroline frequently changed location with its postmaster. Stagecoaches carried the mail later on, dropping it at the tavern or some other stopping place in the community. As rural communities grew and developed, so post offices changed location, and often several would be combined. On July 1, 1902, came the inauguration of rural free delivery; five horse-drawn mail wagons, described as dainty, left the post office in Ithaca to deliver mail to the outlying regions (figure 45). The carriers departed at 9 A.M. sharp and returned at about 4:30 in the afternoon. Many communities in the county today, although not incorporated as villages, still retain their own post offices; they are Brooktondale, Etna, Jacksonville, Ludlowville, McLean, Myers, Newfield, Slaterville Springs, and West Danby.

The first postmaster in Ithaca was appointed by President Jefferson in 1804, and the post office was established in the Dwight Tavern, a "publick house" on the southwest corner of Owego (now State) and Tioga streets. The Ithaca Post Office later rented space in the public library put up by Ezra Cornell. Between 1882 and 1910 it was located in the Colonial Building on the Ithaca Commons. Free mail delivery to residents' homes was begun in September of 1888, the year that Ithaca became a city. The first airmail flight left Tompkins County Airport in September 1948 (figure 46). The present post office building, designed by Federal architect James Knox Taylor, was erected in 1908.

Ithaca got telegraph service in 1846, one of the first communities

45. Rural Free Delivery (1902). From the Ithaca Post Office, located at the time in the Colonial Building on State Street, the mail wagons are preparing to make their deliveries.

in the United States to do so. In the 1840s Ezra Cornell was contracted to lay telegraph wire for Samuel F. B. Morse, and for ten years he built and developed telegraph systems. Nor was Ithaca behind the times for telephone service. The same year that Alexander Graham Bell invented and patented the telephone (1876), Professor William Anthony of the Cornell Physics department, the same professor who built an electric dynamo and put up the arc lights on the campus, got two telephones for purposes of experimentation. He set up one in his lab and the other in his home, on the east side of College Avenue just above State Street. He invited Ithacans to come and have a look at the new gadget, and very soon

46. Tompkins County Airport. The first airmail flight left the airport on September 19, 1948. Air travel, for people as well as freight and mail, plays an increasingly important role today.

people were subscribing. Each subscriber had a key and a telephone, and a connection into what amounted to one big party line, which was at first a telegraph line between the university and downtown. In the late 1870s Professor Anthony started the first private telephone company with William O. Wyckoff, who served as secretary-treasurer while Anthony was manager, mechanic, installer, and improviser. He set up the first switchboard on the top floor of a building on North Tioga Street. The first telephone was an awkward, one-piece unit, with the same opening for listening and speaking. Service was offered day and night, and the first operators were men. Obtaining service was simple; the telephone was installed on a trial basis and if it was considered acceptable, the customer was asked to pay $2 per month. By June 1880 the company had one hundred subscribers, and two years later the New York & Pennsylvania Telephone and Telegraph Company (part of the Bell system and later New York Telephone) bought out Anthony and Wyckoff for a reported $7,000. The first long-distance line connected Ithaca and Auburn in 1883, and in 1887 the company hired two women as operators. A second company, part of the Federal Telephone Company (a rival to the Bell system), was started in 1902 but was bought out by New York Telephone in 1918. The company occupied its own buildings, first at 121 West State and then at 212–220 North Tioga Street, from about 1911 until the early 1980s when it moved to a modern location on East State Street.

This story of transportation and communication once again illustrates Tompkins County's determination to overcome its isolation from commercial centers and its difficult terrain. The railroad companies in particular persisted in their plans to provide adequate transport of people and goods. Some solutions were piecemeal and inadequate; consistent effort and a certain vision were never lacking, however. And the solutions that worked so often resulted from local sustained interest and special ingenuity, as was the case of Anthony's telephone line, for example. This same creativity, dedication, and willingness to invest time and energy in important causes will be seen in the founding and functioning of the county's educational and social institutions.

[4]

Institutions, Organizations, Agencies

TOMPKINS COUNTY, it is said, plays host to more organizations, action groups, clubs, and service agencies, not to mention educational and religious institutions, than any other similar place in the country. For an upstate county, away from both the great East Coast urban belt and the larger cities to the north and west, Tompkins County has an amazing number of educational institutions, and from its first years, the county has abounded with church organizations, small schools, libraries, and benevolent societies as well as some unusual experiments in learning and service.

Education

Higher education is big business in Tompkins County, with a major university, a well-established four-year college with graduate programs, a community college, and various extension programs from outside institutions. Our region fairly teems with all sorts of instructional facilities—private schools, schools in the arts, leading public schools, and many adult education programs. An enormous amount of teaching and learning is part of daily life here.

Cornell University. As the county's largest and richest institution, Cornell University from its site "far above Cayuga's waters" dominates much of our region. The university directly employs a significant number of the county's residents, and the work of many others is related to the university community and its need for services. And the story of Cornell is in many ways representative of our county's particular flavor—industrious people of unusual vision and talent have come together in a spirit of determination, adventure, and adaptability. Cornell's place today, among the leading American universities, is due in large part to continuing dedication to combine learning with life, the academic with the practical.

A farm boy named Ezra Cornell came on foot to Ithaca in 1828, seeking work; he was twenty-one years old, and his only possessions, as he later reported, were tied in a handkerchief. He worked first as a carpenter and then as a mechanic in Otis Eddy's cotton mill (located on the hill where Cascadilla Hall now stands). Very soon he became the mechanic, later the manager of the plaster and flour mills belonging to Colonel Jeremiah S. Beebe at the foot of Ithaca Falls. Cornell blasted a tunnel through the rock wall of the gorge near the falls to provide more efficient waterpower, and ten years later he built a dam above Triphammer Falls, enclosing Beebe Lake to make a reservoir for dry seasons. After the 1837 panic Beebe had to sell his mills and Cornell was out of a job; he worked in various small businesses, did some farming, and speculated in real estate.

In 1842 he left Ithaca. Hired by Samuel F. B. Morse to lay telegraph pipe, for ten years he built and invested in telegraph systems. He returned to Ithaca in 1853 as Ezra Cornell, Esq., the director and largest single stockholder of the Western Union Telegraph Company. He bought the DeWitt farm on the hill between the Cascadilla and Fall Creek gorges (a farm he had eyed years earlier); he called it Forest Park and turned it into a model farm. In 1861 he was elected to the New York State Assembly as a Republican and walked to Albany to take his seat. Already interested in education, and particularly agricultural education, he became president of the state agricultural society. Wanting to do something useful with his very large fortune, as his first project he built and endowed a public library for Ithaca and Tompkins County. Elected to the state senate in 1863, he returned with a draft of the bill to incorporate the Cornell Library in his pocket.

Institutions, Organizations, Agencies

47. Ezra Cornell (1807–1874). The university's founder is seated in the "President's chair," a gift to the university by President White for formal occasions.

At this point he encountered Andrew Dickson White, who had been born in Homer, only twenty-five miles from Cornell's boyhood home in DeRuyter, N.Y., but under very different circumstances (figures 47 and 48). White had studied in Europe and had gained considerable diplomatic experience at an early age; he had also been professor of history at the University of Michigan, a new, free, and to American eyes highly unconventional institution. White had come home to serve in the state assembly, and in his head was the idea for a new university. He had recently inherited a large fortune from his father. He was enlightened, intellectual, and in possession of exceptional organizational gifts (espe-

48. Andrew Dickson White (1832–1918). Cornell University's first president appears here in full academic splendor.

cially in the management of money). In the assembly he was appointed to the Committee on Literature, which dealt with education, and hence came to review Cornell's library incorporation bill. White was impressed by Cornell's generosity—this $100,000 gift to the people of Tompkins County—but even more by, in his words, a "certain breadth and largeness in his way of making it."[10]

Over several years the two men met and began to plan. Though from very different backgrounds, they shared a hunger for scientific knowledge, a sense of destiny, and extraordinary organizational skills.

The United States had long known a real need for scientific education in agriculture. The first concrete suggestion for an agricultural college came from none other than Simeon DeWitt, who in

1819 had published a pamphlet on the necessity of agricultural education in both theory and method for the children of the landed gentry. He wanted enlightened farming to be viewed as an honorable profession on a level with the church, law, and medicine. The agricultural college idea took hold in the state legislature, and various proposals were made between 1830 and 1850. It was not until April of 1853, however, that a charter was granted for the New York State Agricultural College, to be erected in Ovid; Ezra Cornell became one of its trustees. The college never got started, however, and the site later was used for the Willard State Hospital.

Then in 1862 the U.S. Congress passed the Morrill Land Grant Act, which provided for a federal grant of public lands to the states as an endowment for education in agriculture and in the mechanical arts. In the several years that followed, Cornell and White came to an agreement about the university they wanted to start. Cornell proposed the location of an agricultural college in Ithaca and for this purpose would donate his farm of 300 acres, erect on it suitable buildings, and endow the institution with $300,000—on the condition that the state legislature grant Morrill funds to the college. The state charter was granted to Cornell in 1865, and the location of the new school was fixed on the hill in Ithaca. Ezra Cornell had the vision of a large college with at least fifty buildings and thousands of students. It was to have a thoroughly democratized curriculum and be totally nonsectarian. Cornell and White worked hard and well together to establish this university, which was to become unique among institutions of higher learning, in that it combined a privately endowed college with New York State's land grant institution. Diversity was thus integral to the university from the beginning, a diversity that reflected the talents and interests of its two founders. Cornell worked on the land and the buildings and started obtaining the needed equipment, while White drew up the by-laws (an enormous plan of organization) and went about recruiting some of the finest faculty in the Western world. Some 2,000 students applied in response to letters of invitation, and inauguration of the university was held on October 7, 1868, around a rough wooden structure near the present Uris Library. Music was played on the new chimes, a gift of Jennie McGraw and housed temporarily in the wooden building, and 412 students—

49. An Early View of Cornell. This view of the Arts Quadrangle in the early 1870s shows the outline of Sage College and Sage Chapel in the background and on the right the Stone Row. To the left is Sibley Hall. The chimes given by Jennie McGraw, first housed in the tower of McGraw Hall, were moved to the library tower in 1891. The first plantings in front of the Stone Row are yet to be put in.

332 freshmen and 80 upperclassmen—started out in their new venture.

Conscious attempts were made to have beautiful buildings to fit the unusually beautiful natural setting—"this *Universe*" in the words of one enthusiastic orator[11]—but few people found them so. In the words of Goldwin Smith, "Nothing can redeem them but dynamite."[12] In reality the early buildings are handsome structures—grey and somewhat austere perhaps, but stately and dignified (figures 12 and 49). Cascadilla Hall (erected on the site of the old Eddy cotton factory for original use as a sanatorium with water cure, figure 50) became the early center of college life; it provided housing and dining facilities for students and faculty, as well as some office space, and was described by Goldwin Smith as a "great stone barrack" and by White as "repulsive, ill-vented, ill-smelling and uncomfortable" (certainly a far cry from its present state after a recent $7.2 million renovation).[13]

Institutions, Organizations, Agencies

50. Cascadilla Hall (c. 1867). This early photograph shows Cascadilla Hall, originally intended as a sanatorium under the direction of Dr. Samantha Nivison, soon after its completion. The building was taken over by the university before 1868.

The key idea in Ezra Cornell's thinking was to combine study with work—to have a strong-backed, keen-minded group of students who would benefit from self-help. The idea did not work ultimately, though the concept is alive today in the Cornell Tradition Program. The student body nonetheless proved rough and ready and eager to learn. A letter dated January 29, 1872, described the early scene: "Its quite a sight to see 600 or 700 young men going to and from the College building[s] every day. There are 5 very large Stone College buildings and another very large building used as a Laboratory. The College buildings are about a mile all the way up a monstrous hill from the Town."[14] Tuition was only $10 a term, but those in student housing ate terrible food, lived in rooms lit by gas, and used outdoor privies. Many students lived in private residences on the hill or downtown, and by 1876 an omnibus service (taking half an hour) operated six times a day between the campus and the Clinton House.

The original charter written by White omitted references to co-education and to the masculine gender, thus making it applicable to both men and women. The first female student arrived in 1870; she had to lodge in the town and walk the hill several times a day. With the onset of winter she resigned. In June of the following year Henry W. Sage (a native of Ithaca and trustee of Cornell who gave many gifts to the university, including its chapel) offered to erect and endow a separate college for women; it opened in September 1875 with thirty women enrolled and bore his name.

Following his original and basic wish for an outstanding faculty, White went out to find them. He got a reluctant Goldwin Smith from Oxford who, upon seeing some photographs of the region which White had sent him, was reported to have said, "There seem to be a great number of waterfalls, which I abhor." But Smith came anyway and with his classical English education he charmed and gained the respect of his less urbane American colleagues. White also got British historian Henry Morse Stephens, and as he left for one recruiting trip to Europe, Ezra Cornell, who had come to see him off, shouted after the departing ship, "Don't forget the horse doctor!" He didn't, and brought back James Law of Edinburgh, one of Britain's leading pioneers in veterinary science. This coup led to the establishment of the New York School of Veterinary Medicine in 1894. Throughout the university many early courses were taught by eminent visitors, some of whom stayed on.

Outstanding among the early faculty of Cornell was Liberty Hyde Bailey, who became dean of the College of Agriculture in 1903 and profoundly influenced the growth and development of the college and its research. In 1904 he persuaded the state legislature to make the College of Agriculture a state institution while at the same time remaining part of a privately endowed university. As dean he invited Martha Van Rensselaer to come to Cornell; he wanted her to develop a program to teach farm wives to improve home and family conditions (figure 51). Martha Van Rensselaer's work in the home economics department at Cornell (as well as with the Home Conservation Division of the U.S. Food Administration in Washington) led to the founding of the College of Home Economics in 1925, which in 1969 was renamed the College of Human Ecology. The extension and research activities of the col-

Institutions, Organizations, Agencies

51. Home Economics at Cornell. Martha Van Rensselaer is shown in 1905 teaching a cooking class in the basement of Morrill Hall.

lege have seen tremendous growth (in 1984 its research budget alone was $14 million).

Ezra Cornell died in 1874, and A. D. White resigned the presidency in 1885. When Jacob Gould Schurman retired as president in 1920 after a tenure of twenty-eight years, the university had added veterinary, agriculture, medical, and forestry colleges (this last moved rather rapidly to Syracuse in 1912 and today is part of the State University of New York), enrollment had grown from 1,538 to 5,765 and the university's land holdings from 200 to 1,465 acres. It was during Schurman's time in office that Cornell became a great university, and under each successive president Cornell has expanded its facilities and educational offerings. The College of

[119]

Law became the graduate Cornell Law School in 1925; the School of Hotel Administration was created soon thereafter.

To the original small group of buildings dominated by the McGraw Hall tower housing Jennie McGraw's bells that rang out over the campus each day (the chimes mechanism was moved to its present place in the library tower in 1891), the university had added an enormous number and variety of different buildings, its campus reflecting the increasing diversity of American higher education and Cornell's major role in education and research.

Ithaca College. W. Grant Egbert (figure 52), the founder of the Ithaca Conservatory of Music—which was later to become Ithaca College—grew up near Danby. At twenty-three he was studying violin in Berlin at the Königliche Hochschüle für Musik (one of five foreign students to win a place there), and all the time he had in his mind the idea of founding in Ithaca such a conservatory. Ithaca's beauty, refinement, and culture appealed to him; after his return and with the help of Max Gutstadt, a former Syracuse University music student living in Ithaca and also a violinist, he started the school in September 1892 in four rooms in the Day House, 403 East Seneca Street. The school began with eight teachers, including Mrs. Egbert (who had also studied at the Berlin conservatory), and offered instruction in voice, violin, and piano, as well as in several other instruments, foreign languages, elocution, and fencing. Enrollment the first year was 125 students, and the early years saw considerable financial difficulties. Egbert brought in several able administrators to manage the conservatory, including Charles E. Treman. Most influential among them was George C. Williams, who had come from Nebraska and who served as general manager for twenty-five years and then as president.

The conservatory moved within Ithaca several times and between 1894 and 1911 occupied the second and third floors of the old Wilgus Block (into which Rothschild's had moved in 1889, figure 9). The school held its recitals, and later its plays, in the block's Music Hall. In 1909 Jacob Rothschild purchased the Wilgus Block to expand his store, and the conservatory again had to move. After purchasing Judge Douglass Boardman's house on East Buffalo Street in 1910 (it became the administration building),

Institutions, Organizations, Agencies

52. W. Grant Egbert (1869–1928).

the school settled in the DeWitt Park area in 1911, adding a theater building, an administration annex, a library, and a classroom-office building, thus making a campus there (figure 53). The music school expanded by establishing affiliated schools, later to be incorporated: the Williams School of Expression and Dramatic Art was added in 1898, the Ithaca Institution of Public School Music in 1910, the Ithaca School of Physical Education in 1916, and the

53. Ithaca Conservatory of Music Campus. Several of the conservatory's buildings are seen here from DeWitt Park. The Boardman House (also figure 7) is on the right and attached to the back of it are the Little Theatre (built around 1913) and an administration annex (completed in 1924). At the far left is the First Baptist Church steeple.

Ithaca School of Band Instruments (under the direction of world-famous band leader Patrick Conway) in 1922. The Westminster Choir School came in 1929 as an affiliated school but stayed only three years before moving to Princeton, N.J.

The New York State Board of Regents approved the awarding of bachelor's degrees in music, physical education, and oral English in 1925, granted the school a new charter in 1926 with incorporation, and in 1931 approved a plan for combining the seven divisions of the conservatory and affiliated schools into three departments. At this point the Ithaca Conservatory of Music became Ithaca College.

During the years that followed the college struggled, and various projects for the expansion of facilities failed to materialize. Instead, the school adapted downtown commercial buildings and

Institutions, Organizations, Agencies

houses—two old movie theaters became gymnasium facilities, for example, and the residence at 2 Fountain Place became the president's house (it remains so today). In 1945 a director of graduate studies was appointed, and in 1949 land was acquired just outside the city limits, on Danby Road. A fund-raising drive for a gymnasium on the site was set off in 1951.

For a while there was serious consideration of a campus site on Quarry Street, the location of the former hospital buildings purchased by the college in the late 1950s and put to use as dormitories and a science utility building. But in the autumn of 1959 plans were announced for a new campus, to cost $15 million (a figure that soon doubled). Aiding in these plans was an unusual group called the Friends of Ithaca College, which was organized in the early 1950s with the idea of signing up local people to give $100 a year to the college. The Friends organization caught on and grew into a tremendous community effort that raised over $1 million. The cornerstone for the new college union, named for W. Grant Egbert, was laid in 1960, and the building was opened in the fall of 1961 along with five dormitories. The 1960s saw an active and rapid building program, which created with amazing speed a complete modern campus, affording one of the county's most stunning vistas (figure 54). Ithaca College today offers both graduate and undergraduate degrees, with specialities in applied music, television and communication studies, physical education and therapy. Its concerts and theater productions are an important part of Ithaca's cultural scene.

Tompkins Cortland Community College. The county's newest and increasingly visible educational institution is its community college, which first opened in 1968 in an old Smith Corona office building in Groton. Construction of a giant 360,000-square-foot building, with each floor covering about four acres, began in 1972 and was completed for the summer session of 1974. The college is located in the town of Dryden on a tract of 226 acres; the land was purchased with the help of several friends and local civic organizations and developed with public funds provided by the State University of New York and the counties of Tompkins and Cortland. Federal funds were also used in the construction of the building.

Part of the SUNY system, TC3 offers a university-parallel cur-

54. Ithaca College. This view of the modern campus looks toward the south. From left to right are Science Hall, the East and West towers (predominantly dormitories) with the Muller Faculty Center between them, Muller Chapel, and the Friends Hall (named for the Friends of Ithaca College) and Job Hall (both administration buildings). (Photograph by Jon Crispin, courtesy of Ithaca College)

riculum so that students after two years can transfer to a four-year college; vocational courses oriented toward careers in business, mechanics, industry, and health care; a "cooperative" system whereby a student can work one semester, study one semester. It provides night courses, summer sessions, and on occasion contract courses in which the college sets up a particular program or workshop that businesses have requested. The student body numbers 3,500 today, and its average age is twenty-six years. The total professional staff is 100, with another 100 serving as adjunct faculty.

This "people's college" was started by a group of citizens in the two counties who saw a need for advanced career education. The community college's purpose is to provide informal, nontraditional education—services that exist nowhere else—and to give people job training, or help them retrain when their work skills become obsolete. The school is open to all and provides an opportunity to learn for students who, for various reasons, do not fit elsewhere. With its versatility it can teach individuals according to their abilities, giving instruction that ranges from the remedial to the highly sophisticated.

TC3 has become a leader in certain domains—the nursing program is ranked one of the top ten in the country—and it offers up-to-date courses in the high-technology field. In the years ahead it will probably look to programs in international affairs and manpower training for global businesses. In the words of its founding president, Hushang Bahar, who came to Ithaca twenty years ago to be dean of the Ithaca College Graduate School and who has led TC3 from its opening, the function of TC3 is mass education, and the community college must really be the college of and for democracy.

Private Schools. Some of the county's early communities offered private secondary schooling to their residents. As early as 1800 Trumansburg had a private school for a short time. The Ithaca Academy, a private school built partly with public funds, was begun in 1819 on the site of the present DeWitt Building (a site first used for a school in 1807) and finally completed in 1826; a new brick building was added in 1840 (figure 55). In early times it had dormitories for boarders. By 1842 it had 281 students and three departments, one of which was established by direction of the Board of Regents to provide training for "common school" teachers. It was one of several private schools in the county still in existence in the 1870s, and a letter from 1872 reports that it had 300 students at that time.[15] In 1874, when the state established a system of graded public schools, the academy's buildings and facilities were leased to the Ithaca Board of Education, which first used them for both a grammar and a high school. The school board purchased the academy property in 1879, and it became the public high school. This same pattern can be seen elsewhere in the county. The Dryden Academy (first opened there in 1862 and also known as the Dryden Seminary), Groton's private school (founded in 1837), and the Trumansburg Academy (which opened in 1855) all became part of the public school systems of their villages in 1872. Indeed, the

55. Ithaca Academy. The picture shows the school's newer brick building, erected around 1840. Behind it stands the original wooden structure completed in 1826. The academy became Ithaca's high school in 1879.

Trumansburg Academy was given to the district as a gift (figure 56). The usual practice was for the private school (buildings, staff, and all) to be converted into the public high school.

The Cascadilla School was founded in Ithaca in 1870 by Lucian Wait, who at that time had charge of the mathematics department at Cornell, to prepare students for entrance into the university. Headquartered for a while at Cascadilla Hall (figure 50), it became

56. Trumansburg Academy. Built in 1855, the building burned in 1892.

a four-year high school accepting boarding students, then a day preparatory school, and then ceased operations for a while. In 1946 the brick building at Oak and Summit avenues on East Hill was bought by Maxwell Kendall, who started the school up again. With accreditation from SUNY and the Board of Regents, Cascadilla offers programs for its fifty regular students, of whom half are boarders, and gives public high school students of the area the opportunity to take courses—some of them accelerated—in preparation for college. It has a program for foreign students with emphasis on learning English and a summer session that has been in existence for sixty years.

Ithaca's Immaculate Conception parochial school opened in 1884, in a building on West Buffalo Street. Six nuns from the Sisters of St. Joseph taught that first year, and the order has run the school ever since. The original building was expanded with a four-room addition, but a fire in April 1946 destroyed a large part of the school. Funds were raised to build a new school, which was completed in 1947. In 1955 more classrooms and a cafeteria were added, and in 1965 a parish hall was built that included a gymnasium/auditorium. The parochial school provides instruction for Grades 1 through 8 and now employs some lay teachers.

The 1970s and 1980s have brought renewed interest in private schooling and with it the establishment of Hickory Hollow and the Baptist Bible Church School in Newfield, the School of the Finger Lakes in Danby, the Mayer School in Ithaca, and the Montessori Elementary and Secondary School of Ithaca. Several independent schools offer courses in the arts, and programs are available at the three-county Board of Cooperative Educational Services (BOCES), which provides vocational and extension courses in its new facility on Warren Road in the town of Ithaca, as well as at Cornell's Experimental College and at the Women's Community Building in downtown Ithaca.

Ithaca also had a higher level vocational school for a number of years. In 1876 one of the first business schools in the country was set up by William O. Wyckoff, in the old Titus Block on State Street. Wyckoff was a supreme court reporter and needed someone to copy his notes (which he had taken in shorthand). He asked his neighbor, Mary Adsitt, to do this job and provided her with a typewriter; she quickly learned both typing and stenography and soon was in great demand all over the state. Wyckoff saw the need for a typing and stenography school, and once it was started, students came from far and wide, moving out into the large local job market after their training. The school became the Practical Business School, and in the early 1900s its chief assistant was hired to teach typing and stenography in the high school curriculum. It was incorporated into Ithaca College in 1945. Today business and related instruction is offered by Learning Foundations of Ithaca.

George Junior Republic. This unusual educational community is located on 1,200 acres in Freeville and today has about 150 resident young men and women. It was started in the 1890s by William R. George, a native of Dryden known as Daddy George, who brought a group of young people up from New York City to a summer camp in Freeville as part of the *New York Herald Tribune* "fresh air" program. George Junior Republic was founded in 1895 as an outgrowth of this project and is designed to teach adolescents citizenship, self-government, and how to accept responsibility in the community. With the school under the New York State education department, students are referred through county departments of social services and through the courts. They are categorized not as juvenile delinquents but as persons "in need of supervision." The republic offers secondary school education and vocational training, and it provides work/study programs. Faculty work with the students on a one-to-one basis. On the grounds there are about thirty buildings, including offices and classrooms, a large recreational center and dining room, a clinic, and residential buildings for both staff and students; the school also makes use of buildings in nearby communities.

Public Schools. One of the first actions that the early settlers took was to set aside a building for a school. In 1812 Daniel D. Tompkins, then governor of New York State, backed a bill for a complete system of public schools throughout the state. The bill became law that year, and it provided for a public school within walking distance of every child in the state. And so every community, large and small, had at least one school, usually accommodating children from grades 1 to 12 in one room. Because of the number of classes taught together, and because a school had to be within walking distance of every child, there were a considerable number of these one-room schoolhouses through most of the nineteenth century (figure 57). Students in the early days were taught the basics, the three Rs, and because most of them lived and worked on the farms, the school year was short. During the summer months the children were at home working the land, and during much of the winter the weather kept them away from school. According to contemporary reports, much of early education was lamentable. Several early schoolhouses still stand, the most notable being Dryden's Eight-Square Schoolhouse, built in 1827.

The first school in Ithaca, District School No. 16, was built on the corner of Seneca and Cayuga streets, site of the DeWitt Building and a corner that has always had school buildings on it. In 1817 some wild elements of the populace burned it down. A new school was built on the site, and in 1823 the Ithaca Academy was incorporated there. In 1825 the district sold its interest in the school build-

57. Old Schoolhouse. This school, District School No. 5, was located south of Applegate Corners in Enfield and was one of many small schoolhouses in the county.

ing to the academy and began constructing its separate public school on the northwest corner of Geneva and Mill (now Court) streets, opened in 1828. Called the central public schoolhouse, it was replaced in 1854 with a larger building, and a system of grades supplanted the old Lancastrian "forms."

When the state legislature enacted the union school district law in 1874, consolidating the public schools in the different townships into school districts, private academies were generally leased to the public school system. The village of Ithaca elected twelve commissioners and all the public schools were placed under their jurisdiction. By autumn of 1874 West Hill School had been erected and small temporary schools had been opened on East and South hills. Several other schools had been built by the turn of the century. The high school took over the old academy building in 1875; a new school later built on that site (figure 58) burned in 1912 and was replaced by yet another high school building (the present DeWitt Building), completed in 1914 and until 1932 the location of both the junior and the senior highs. In 1960 the present high school was opened on a 46-acre tract between Cayuga and Lake streets, and two new junior high schools followed. The DeWitt

Institutions, Organizations, Agencies

58. Ithaca High School. This building replaced the old Ithaca Academy buildings in 1884. Grammar school classes were held on the first floor and high school classes on the second. In the background is the present First Presbyterian Church, built in 1900.

Building has since been redesigned to accommodate a basement mall, offices, and apartments.

With the Public School Act of 1874 different towns of the county formed their own school districts. In 1956 most of Enfield became a part of the Ithaca school district. In 1931 the town of Danby still had fourteen schools operating, but today it too is part of the Ithaca system. The Newfield central district was formed in 1938 and until recently the school system was the town's biggest employer and the only business with an annual turnover of more than $1 million. In both 1962 and 1965 Newfield residents voted against a merger with the Ithaca district. Trumansburg consolidated its schools into the Union School in 1844 and opened its own private academy in 1855. From 1878 grades 1–8 were taught in the Union Free School with the academy serving the district as the high school. When the old academy burned in 1892, a new school building was erected and housed all the grades in one building. It too burned in 1924 and was replaced. Trumansburg's district was formed in 1928; a new elementary school was built in 1955 and a new high school in 1961.

Schools in the nineteenth century and well into the twentieth were a far cry from those of today. They must have been very crowded; James Rawlins, an English visitor to Ithaca in October 1873, describes the public school, which he found "in rather poor building of wood (for this country), with about 700 children."[16] In addition to their small size, they offered only a limited curriculum and activities. A typical day in the early 1900s in Ithaca began at 9 A.M. with opening exercises, which included verses from the Bible, a song or two, and quotations, followed by reading and arithmetic until noon. In the afternoon short classes were held in writing, grammar, geography, elementary history, spelling, drawing, and physiology. There were two recesses of fifteen minutes, one in the morning and the other in the afternoon, and one hour for lunch. Dismissal was at 4 P.M. The last half-hour on Friday was given over to spelling bees, counting games, or a special story. The school year ended early in May, and exams from the fourth grade up came from the Regents in Albany. According to an account of the West Hill School in the 1900s, only two or three grades were taught there, as West Hill was sparsely settled. Pupils went downtown to school for the sixth grade and above. There was no running water or plumbing in the school; a pump stood outside and "other facilities" decorated the corners of the school property.[17]

Libraries

A few early communities in Tompkins County had their own public libraries, opened soon after the settlements had been started. The Ulysses Philomathic Library was founded by 1811, the same year that the village of Trumansburg got its name. The library

Institutions, Organizations, Agencies

59. Southworth Library, Dryden. This small and charming library was given to the village by Jennie McGraw Fiske and has a notable collection of historical documents and papers.

functioned until 1839, when all its books were sold, and it was not until 1935 that it opened again. It is housed today in an annex at the rear of the Masonic Temple, next door to the First Presbyterian Church of Ulysses on Main Street. The Caroline Library Association was formed in 1818, with $100 pledged for establishing a circulating library, which opened in 1819 with 150 volumes. It continued for ten years. The library in Dryden, named Southworth Library and located on the corner of Library and West Main streets, was a gift to the village from Jennie McGraw Fiske, whose grandfather had been an early settler of the town. Jennie McGraw Fiske used part of her considerable fortune for a library to be named for her mother's family, also early settlers in the Dryden area. The Southworth Library was designed by Ithaca architect William Henry Miller and was constructed of Ohio sandstone in 1894 (figure 59). It possesses an original manuscript of the address Lincoln gave at the time of his reelection in 1864, a gift from Robert Todd Lincoln to Congressman John W. Dwight of Dryden.

The Tompkins County Public Library stands today on the corner of Cayuga and Court streets in Ithaca, across the street from the First Presbyterian Church in DeWitt Park. It is a spacious modern building, constructed in 1968. Local architect J. Victor Bagnardi was selected by the county board to design the new structure, and in keeping with the surroundings Bagnardi planned the curved extension of the library in front to balance the semicircular apse of the Presbyterian Church opposite. The open interior balcony, which contains stacks on all four sides, can be converted into a full second story if needed. The library has a grand total of 120,372 items today, of which 81,047 are books; other holdings include periodicals, disc and cassette recordings, pamphlets, catalogues, maps, and audiovisual equipment. These holdings are now filed on computer. So are those of the regional Finger Lakes Library System, which covers five counties; it was established in 1958, and one year later the Tompkins County Library was designated the central library for the system. The Finger Lakes system rents space in the building, and its holdings, including a large collection of adult nonfiction, are deposited here. The system's Bookmobile and station wagon are garaged at the Tompkins County Library. The library also offers educational programs and plays an important role in Ithaca's community access cable system. The Friends of the Tompkins County Public Library, an incorporated organization of persons interested in books, the library, its facilities, and its needs, held their first meeting in December 1946. The Friends of the Library book sale, now one of the ten largest second-hand book sales in the United States, has been an annual fall event in Tompkins County since 1947.

But all this activity is fairly recent. For years the Tompkins County Public Library operated as a private institution, the Cornell Public Library. When a new library building was proposed in 1957, private supporters were found for the project. But by the early 1960s it became apparent that private funding would not be adequate to the large enterprise, and through the determined efforts of Sherman Peer, a library trustee, and Helen Vanderwort, considerable funds were raised, and the library was taken over by Tompkins County in 1964 and thus received public sponsorship. As was the case for several privately funded institutions, expenses became so great—despite help from the city over the years—that

Institutions, Organizations, Agencies

the library could not function. The county did not operate the library until 1968 when the new building was completed. A chartered county public library today, it is governed by a Board of Trustees, a citizens' group appointed by the Tompkins County Board of Representatives, and staffed by employees of the county.

The first public library in Ithaca had been organized in 1806; its books were the property of the village's literary society, the Ithaca Lyceum (later the Minerva Society at the Ithaca Academy, founded in 1826). The person responsible for the first public library building was, as we have already seen, Ezra Cornell, who bought the lot on the southeast corner of Tioga and Seneca streets and endowed a library building. Building was begun in 1863, and the Cornell Library Association was incorporated by an act of the state legislature on April 5, 1864. The large and imposing three-story structure with a cupola (figure 60), provided space for the library's books and facilities, reading rooms, and a large auditorium called Library Hall, which played host to numerous meetings over the years, including Cornell University's inaugural ceremony and many of its commencements and lectures. Ezra Cornell also left considerable funds for the acquisition of new books.

The public library, with free circulation, was dedicated on a cold December evening in 1866. It was quite an event; during the day the building had been decked out with flags and the auditorium decorated with evergreens, some of which had been fashioned to spell out the founder's name. Despite the weather, which was "intensely cold and inclement," the hall was crowded, and the dedication ceremony began with the firing of guns and the "exultant ringing" of all the village bells. There were the customary prayers and speeches, including one by Ezra Cornell, who gave a history of the construction, a description of the various rooms and their intended use (in addition to library facilities and the 800-seat auditorium, space was designated for a bank, offices, an armory, the post office, the Ithaca Farmers Club, and the Ithaca Historical Society). He also provided a detailed account of costs (rental income from the building was expected to cover operating expenses). He went on to tell his fellow citizens of Ithaca that the property belonged to them and to the citizens of the county.[18] This building was demolished in 1960 in the city's first wave of urban renewal;

[135]

60. Tioga Street Looking South (c. 1900). The Cornell Public Library (to the left) housed the offices of the First National Bank for several years. On the near corner is the statue of Hebe, standing above the drinking fountain erected in 1896 in front of City Hall by the Women's Christian Temperance Union; the statue was later melted down for metal. Opposite the library is the Ithaca Savings Bank building, designed by William Henry Miller and erected in 1887; the present bank building dates from 1924. Next to it are the Tompkins County Trust Company, the County Clerk's office building, the Finch Block (which once housed the Corner Book Store), and the Wilgus Block (across State Street). In the background is the mansion on South Hill of Jane McGraw, third wife of John McGraw and stepmother of Jennie McGraw Fiske.

the library moved to cramped temporary quarters in the Sons of Italy Hall at 417 West State Street and finally to its present location in 1969.

Institutions, Organizations, Agencies

Community Services and Benevolent Societies

The communities of Tompkins County, like their counterparts everywhere, have over the years had to confront crime, poverty, and disease and deal with the consequences of natural disasters — fire and, particularly, flood. And over the years residents have established organizations and devised means for dealing with these different problems. When the early towns were being established, various ordinances for public protection met the questions of legal regulations and fire protection. Each community developed several fire companies, which generally were consolidated later in the century. With the establishment of Tompkins County in 1817 the courthouse and jail were built, setting up an apparatus for the trial and detention of lawbreakers.

In the county's early days, it is reported, there was a great deal of sabbath breaking, gambling, horse racing, drunkenness, licentiousness, and profane swearing;[19] the inebriated were locked in the hog pound to dry out, and moral and temperance societies sprang up all over the county. Ithaca's Moral Society was founded around 1812 by Benjamin Drake, who was called Tecumseh by his followers. Like its contemporary, the Society for the Prevention of Crime, it was designed to enforce certain rules (sometimes created by the society) and protect citizens in the absence of civil authority. Benjamin Joy founded the Lansing Town Temperance Society on New Year's Eve of 1827, at which time Lansing alone had eight distilleries. And in the late 1820s drinking and drunkenness had reached such alarming proportions in "Shin Hollow" that concerned residents of Trumansburg met in 1828 to form a temperance movement, which grew enormously during the great religious revival of the 1830s. When Trumansburg was incorporated as a village in 1872, drunkenness was still a major problem, and the temperance movement still large and influential. Such problems were widespread in the county, for the distillation of alcoholic spirits was a significant industry in the nineteenth century, and in the 1840s gin was even advertised as a remedial agent for medicinal use. In 1898 the city of Ithaca issued forty-six hotel and saloon licenses, and nine pharmacies also had permits to sell liquor. The Women's Christian Temperance Union, which had organized in

1874, put up a drinking fountain in 1896 on the northeast corner of Seneca and Tioga streets in front of the City Hall (figure 60). A statue of Hebe, goddess of youth, stood above the fountain, which was considered an alternative—both literal and figurative—to alcohol and its devastating effects.

Poverty and homelessness were also early problems; many early settlers gave their poor neighbors a helping hand. Throughout the nineteenth century it was common practice for the impoverished to be assigned to the care of the wealthier citizenry. The canal brought in many itinerant, uneducated workers, who in the late nineteenth century formed a squatters' settlement along the Inlet and the west shore of the lake, a separate community of the city's poor. This settlement, a collection of shacks and huts made of packing boxes and rough lumber with tin and sheet-iron roofs, was known as the Silent City (figure 61). It was spread out along the "Rhine" (the inhabitants were called "Rhiners") and survived until about 1910. The settlement was called the Silent City, it is said, because its inhabitants slept by day and fished and poached by night; another version has it that when the police came to break up the frequent drunken brawls, the whole area suddenly became silent as a tomb. Begging was widespread at the end of the century. Here were people in need of work, food, and shelter, a situation that was repeated during the Great Depression.

With the growth and sophistication of modern society have come other problems calling for public and private aid and solutions: unemployment, inadequate and improper nourishment, broken homes, drug abuse, and an ever growing aged population.

Social Services. The Tompkins County Department of Social Services has been operating in an official capacity since the 1930s and the passage of the Social Security Act and other programs of the New Deal. The commissioner of the department in our county is appointed by the county administrator and runs several major programs. One of these, the County Home, has been under the jurisdiction of Tompkins County since it was constructed in the early nineteenth century as a home for the poor. The county's Board of Supervisors voted to establish a Poor House in 1827, and a wooden building was erected in the town of Ulysses, six miles northwest

Institutions, Organizations, Agencies

61. Silent City, Ithaca. This group of buildings along the "Rhine" (the Cayuga Inlet) was photographed in 1895. West Hill is in the background.

of Ithaca. In 1876, 75 persons lived there. In 1892 the building was replaced by a brick structure called the County House, which provided food and shelter for the county's indigent and incapacitated. The insane were taken to the Willard State Hospital, which had been established in the 1870s near Ovid. Today the County Home, located on the original site on Perry City Road, is an adult public home for older citizens, those who do not have special health requirements and can take care of themselves, but who no longer can live alone. Although it has room for 60 people, only 42 (with an average age of 66) are living there now. A staff of 25 maintains the facility.

The Department of Social Services has 130 staff people over and above those who work at the County Home. Its other major programs include income maintenance (public assistance, aid to dependent children and the elderly, home relief, food stamps, Medicaid), the collection and disbursement of court-ordered family support, and child and family services (connected with child abuse and neglect, adoption, and foster care, among others). Tompkins County also maintains separate service agencies such as the Office for the Aging, Human Services and Community Resources, and Environmental Management.

Medicine and Health. Medicine in the nineteenth century was a far cry from what we know today. Knowledge of the human body and disease was so limited that doctors were severely handicapped in their work. Many who practiced learned by apprenticeship and by reading the existing medical texts. County medical societies were established early, in large part because of the need to protect the public from bad doctors and quacks, to regulate medical study, and to examine students and issue licenses. The Tompkins County Medical Society was incorporated in 1818, disbanded in 1844 (for no known reason), and when it was reorganized at the Clinton House in October of 1862, fifty-two physicians signed the constitution and by-laws. The Cornell University Board of Trustees called for organization of a medical department for the university as early as 1866, but it was not until 1898 that the Cornell Medical College was finally established. In that same year a two-year medical preparatory course was offered for the first time.

In the early days of the county, formally trained doctors were few and far between. Two of the county's earliest settlers, Joseph Speed of Caroline and Lewis Beers of Danby, were medical doctors but both were better known in other capacities. Throughout the nineteenth century many doctors in the county lived in hamlets and traveled by horse or carriage to visit their patients. One of the county's earliest physicians was a Dr. Andrews, who lived at Mott's Corners; he manufactured his own medicine and was said to even have made his own tin boxes for it. Dr. Daniel Mead came in 1820 to Slaterville and practiced there for forty years. Edward J. Morgan came to Ithaca in 1844 and established a practice in homeopathy. C. C. Cook, who practiced in Newfield, got a degree from the medical school in Geneva and came in 1845, owning only his horse and medicine case; he became president of the Medical Society in 1866. Patent medicines with such designations as worm tea, vegetable rheumatic drops, and blood purifiers were widely sold. An advertisement in 1870 described Gargling Oil as liniment for man and beast, good for rheumatism, frost bites, flesh wounds, chapped hands, lame back, swellings, tumors, toothaches, and painful nervous afflictions.[20]

The need for more medical facilities in the county concerned many citizens during the second half of the nineteenth century. One particularly active was Dr. Samantha Nivison, who was born in Jacksonville in 1833 and became the first female physician to practice in Tompkins County. (In 1880, when New York State doctors were registered officially, seventeen women physicians were practicing in the county.) With a medical degree from the University of Pennsylvania, she opened an office in 1860 just over the Schuyler County line in Mecklenburg. Her specialty was preventive medicine, and she had considerable experience in self-treatment: she suffered from severe pulmonary problems, for which she found a cure in living a healthy, vigorous, outdoor life. Wanting to put her ideas into practice, in 1862 she purchased the Dryden Springs House, erected in 1845 as a hotel and located near mineral springs discovered in 1820 by Benjamin Lacy (one of the village founders, who was out prospecting for salt). Dr. Nivison renamed the large and rambling structure the Dryden Springs Place and set up a water-cure system for treatments. On her staff were three other medical doctors (who happened to be her two sisters and brother). The establishment, with its luxurious and spacious interior and extended grounds, became a summer resort as well as an invalid home with hospital facilities (figure 62).

With the success of the Dryden facility, Dr. Nivison sought to establish a similar but larger institution in Ithaca. She got the support of Ezra Cornell, who headed the trustees and who obtained incorporation for the establishment. Many Ithacans became stockholders. Dr. Nivison drew up plans, and the building called Cascadilla Place was finished in 1866 (see figure 50). The project lacked sufficient financial support, however, and before 1868 the building was leased to the newly founded university. In 1884 Dr. Nivison

62. Dryden Springs Place. This luxury hotel and water-cure sanatorium had extensive formal grounds with walks, springs, and recreational areas. (Photograph courtesy of Southworth Library)

left the region but the sanatorium in Dryden continued as a summer resort. After 1900 the building was no longer used, and in 1945 it burned.

In January 1889 a group of Ithaca women formed the Hospital Association. The Burt mansion on North Aurora Street at Cascadilla Creek was presented to the association in 1890, and it became the area's first hospital. An adjacent brick building was erected to house the contagious ward and a nurses' home; an annex at the rear of the Burt House provided an operating room. The hospital was filled to capacity during the typhoid epidemic of 1903. The property was sold in 1910, and two years later a new hospital was opened on a four-acre tract on South Quarry Street overlooking Six Mile Creek. At least three additions were made to this structure, and a large private house, given by the family of Josiah B.

Williams, was added for a nursing home. The new building was called the Ithaca City Hospital; it was a private institution, however, sustained by voluntary contributions and endowments. In 1926 the name was changed to the Ithaca Memorial Hospital. Another small hospital with operating facilities, called Conklin Sanatorium, was also in service during the 1930s and 1940s, on North Tioga Street.

In 1948, when the Memorial Hospital took over a TB facility built in 1935 on the Trumansburg Road (the Hermann M. Biggs Hospital), control of the hospital passed to the county. In the late 1950s Ithaca College purchased the old hospital buildings on Quarry Street. The main building was converted into a dormitory, called Quarry, which later became Ithacare Center, a residential care facility for the elderly and handicapped. Tompkins County's modern hospital facility, constructed to the south of the older Biggs Hospital buildings, was opened in May 1980, and since January 1, 1981, it has again been operated as a private facility, owned by a not-for-profit membership corporation, under the name of Tompkins Community Hospital.

Legislation passed by the state in 1832 required that each city and village have a board of health and a physician health official. Ithaca's first Board of Health, established the year before, directed its early attention to ridding the city of unsanitary privies and overflowing cesspools. After Ithaca's incorporation as a city in 1888, the first recorded report of the city's board chiefly expressed concern with the improvement of the environment and control of infectious diseases. The board's report in 1902 gave the leading cause of death as pulmonary consumption. Although typhoid, malaria, and cholera were endemic at the time, there was just a handful of cases of typhoid fever in the city that year—a situation that changed rapidly, for 1,350 cases were reported in 1903. The region was engulfed in an epidemic that served the cause of public health in subsequent years. The epidemic became so serious that Dr. George Soper was sent from New York City by the state commissioner of health to take charge of the situation.

The major problem in Ithaca was its unsanitary water supply. Henry W. Sage in the 1850s had been granted permission to bring in a pure water supply and had put in a water system, but the water to the reservoirs (there were two at the time) came from Six Mile Creek in a state anything but pure. The privies of the town of Caroline put out into the creek, and the remains of dead animals disposed of in the fields along the creek were washed down with each heavy rain. In 1903 there was a flood, and the water stood around for quite a while, becoming increasingly polluted. The privately owned waterworks were surrendered to the city in 1904; the state wrote a sanitary code and fines were imposed for pollution of the water supply. At the same time, first steps were taken to eliminate the swamps. The epidemic was over, but residual cases lingered for another ten years.

The next public health war was against tuberculosis and in 1911 the Ithaca Tuberculosis Association, a private organization, was founded. A farm was rented for the children of TB families during the summer and to strengthen their condition. In 1915 a new building designed to accommodate about thirty children and named the Cayuga Preventorium was constructed northwest of Ithaca to continue this program. Today it has become a nature center. The county remodeled an old hotel on the south side of Taughannock gorge for the care of about thirty TB patients, and this facility continued as the Tompkins County Tuberculosis Hospital until New York State opened the Hermann F. Biggs Memorial Hospital in 1935.

The care of victims of infantile paralysis had started with a small private convalescent hospital founded after the end of World War I and located in the Bostwick home on South Albany Street (figure 63). Mary Hibbard, with the assistance of the public health nurse assigned to the county by the state to provide rehabilitation and training for polio victims, interested others in the project, and they were able to raise enough money to lease the private home. The Infantile Paralysis Home Association was incorporated in 1926, and the Reconstruction Home was built, the first institution in the country dedicated to the rehabilitation of polio victims. Today's successor to the Reconstruction Home for Infantile Paralysis provides care for the elderly as well as general rehabilitation services.

The Tompkins County Health Department was inaugurated in 1947 and serves the entire county. The Mental Health Clinic was founded in the 1950s. The department also provides skilled visiting

Institutions, Organizations, Agencies

63. Bostwick House. This residence on South Albany Street in Ithaca was privately purchased and turned into a polio hospital. The Reconstruction Home was later built on the site.

home health care nurses, well-baby clinics in different areas of the county, monthly orthopedic clinics and a physical therapist who makes home visits, immunizations, and ambulance service.

The dental profession has had a prominent place in the county's history. Solyman Brown, a Swedenborgian preacher and friend of Dr. Lewis Beers, practiced in Danby and Ithaca in the mid-nineteenth century. A leader in the intense struggle to establish dentistry as a profession separate from medicine, he was the co-founder of the *American Journal of Dentistry* and the American Society of Dental Surgeons. Dr. George W. Melotte, internationally known dentist and the inventor of Melotte's metal still used in dentistry today, held nine separate patents for dental appliances and apparatus. He came to Ithaca in 1866 and practiced until 1883; Melotte's Dental Cottage was located on the present site of the Tompkins County Trust Company.

The Tompkins County Dental Society was organized in 1909

and has been active ever since in establishing and strengthening the profession in the region.

Private Organizations. The most important group of private organizations are the churches, described below, but many communities in the county have formed societies to benefit other people and to provide community service. The temperance and moral societies, as mentioned before, started up already in the 1820s and continued their activities throughout the century. The Masons established their lodges first in Caroline in 1808, then in Trumansburg in 1818; the Lansing Masons organized between 1824 and 1828. Between 1830 and 1850 anti-Masonic feeling ran high, and membership dwindled; most lodges were revived after 1850. Of the well-known fraternal orders, the Odd Fellows, the Elks, the Lions, the Moose, the Eagles have had active chapters in our region. In the year 1879, it was reported, twelve different secret societies flourished in Ithaca. And organizations with an orientation toward people in business and commerce, Rotary International and the Kiwanis Club, have their local chapters and have been involved for years in various service projects. The Salvation Army founded its local chapter in 1892, the American Legion its local post in 1919. The Boy Scouts got started in 1914, the Campfire Girls in 1910, the Girl Scouts in 1919. Most of these organizations are well and active today, and to them have been added myriads of others, many associated with the churches and the college campuses, others designed to administer to local needs, such as the Family and Children's Service, Challenge Industries (which provides a sheltered workshop for the mentally disabled and the physically handicapped), and Meadow House (a drug rehabilitation residence). Tompkins County residents help fund many of these organizations through contributions to an annual comprehensive and coordinated fund drive, the United Way.

In the second half of the nineteenth century many benevolent organizations came into existence, often through the efforts and concern of dedicated women. The first of these was the Ladies' Voluntary Aid Society, started in 1861 to collect clothing for soldiers fighting in the Civil War, but the most significant was the Ladies' Union Benevolent Society. Started in 1869, it was incorporated in

1870 and then given an endowment by the state legislature. Jane McGraw, third wife of John McGraw, donated a three-story house on South Aurora Street to provide space for elderly women with no close family to care for them; from this idea came the modern McGraw House, a residence for retired persons on South Geneva Street.

Elizabeth Beebe's contribution was probably the most far reaching. In the 1880s she worked to obtain help for the impoverished people who lived in the Inlet section of the city; she got the churches to help and obtained a lot west of the Lehigh Valley Station to build a mission house called the Inlet Mission, which held religious services on Sunday mornings. A wooden chapel built from the original mission and called Beebe Chapel (figure 64) stood at the intersection of Buffalo and State streets; it was eventually torn down. The Children's Home, incorporated in 1889 and run by Elizabeth Beebe personally for many years, was established on land and buildings donated to the Benevolent Society by Edward Esty and located on West Seneca Street. The original structure was replaced by a brick building in 1909; its stained glass window survives in the DeWitt Historical Society. There was also the settlement house, providing a place for some poor persons to live; located on West State Street in a former granary, it later became West Side House. The Social Service League, incorporated in 1906, purchased the property and the West Side House, which continued as a settlement house until 1916. It was torn down to make way for the new flood control channel.

Early in the 1900s, four women's clubs in Ithaca—the Political Study Club (later the Tompkins County League of Women Voters), the Women's Christian Temperance Union (which had held its first meetings in 1874), the Ithaca Women's Club (founded by Louise Lord Riley with every fourth meeting devoted to women's rights issues), and the Cornell University Campus Club—got together. They formed Ithaca's City Federation of Women's Organizations, which would attempt to improve the educational, recreational, philanthropic, health, and civic climate in both city and county. Their first project was to rent a building to be used as a resting place for farm women who had come to town for the day. In 1920 the group was able to purchase the Winton House, a Sec-

64. Beebe Mission House. Elizabeth Beebe's organization was founded in 1882 as the Inlet Mission. The west end of State Street diagonally crosses the picture, with Floral Avenue coming in on the right. To the left of the mission house is Buffalo Street and in the background is the end of the railroad station.

ond Empire residence belonging to the Miller family and located on the corner of Seneca and Cayuga streets. The building was opened on January 1, 1921, as the Women's Community Building; it was used for clubs and groups and for women's social activities, as well as providing quarters, a kitchen, and a laundry for young women. These facilities were expanded in 1926 with the purchase of an adjacent building.

In the urban renewal of the late 1950s and early 1960s Winton House was demolished. In 1959 the new Women's Community Building, designed by local architects Tallman & Tallman, was built on the same site, mortgaged, and paid for (with special funds raised for the purpose) by 1960. Today the federation has 46 member clubs (including several men's organizations), and the Women's Community Building with its professional staff provides meeting places for these member clubs, a dormitory for about twenty young women, an emergency transient room for women, and a wide variety of educational and cultural programs. In the basement is housed the Service League store, where used clothing is bought and sold on consignment; proceeds benefit local mental health programs.

Churches and Religious Organizations

Every early settlement in the county had at least one religious group that met and worshiped together. The first church services were held in private homes, but very soon the groups were organizing and building churches. They reflected very clearly the vigor and the independence of this young society: the one feature common to all the early religious organizations was that the laity came together and established their principles as a first step; then, and only then, did they ask a clergyman to come and be their leader. In those early days the feeling was strongly held that religion was needed in the new and rather rough young settlements. Reports from Ithaca, from Lansing, from Trumansburg spoke of ungodly communities, where morals were loose, tempers high, drink ubiquitous, and Sunday services ignored. In the early 1800s, it was said, Ithaca was a "wicked place."

The Presbyterians established the first formal church in the village of Ithaca (they organized as early as 1804, with thirteen members, and installed their first minister in 1805). In Trumansburg they first met in 1803 and built their church (on the site of the present Greek Revival First Presbyterian Church of Ulysses, erected in

65. Danby Federated Church (c. 1890).

1850) in 1817/9. They organized in Dryden in 1808. The Reverend Wisner, with the Reverend Samuel Parker, organized the church in Ludlowville in 1817.

Other denominations soon started up and built their churches. The Methodists held their first meetings in Lansing as early as 1794; they built their Red Meeting House on the Asbury Road in 1811. The Methodists were the first to organize in Newfield. The first church organization in Caroline (dating from about 1812) was the Reformed Dutch Church, under the leadership of the Reverend Garret Mandeville. The Baptists were the first to organize in the villages of Etna and Enfield and in what they called the progressive and promising village of Danby, in the "healthy highlands" above and away from the malarial swamps of Cayuga Lake. The first church building in the county still standing today is the Danby Federated Church, erected in 1813 (figure 65). Also in Danby was the Church of New Jerusalem, formed under the care of Swedenborgian preacher Dr. Lewis Beers, and built in 1825.

The Presbyterian church was the predominant congregation in Ithaca all through the nineteenth century. Its strength was due in part to the early presence of a compellingly strong minister, the Reverend William Wisner, who arrived in February 1816 to take over a small, disorganized group. He first preached in a small schoolhouse (some reports say a loft), but by 1818 there was a new church building on the corner of Court (then Mill) and Cayuga streets, which faced the park and which was enlarged in 1825 to accommodate a congregation of 260 members. The congregation was to increase fourfold during the 1820s as religion became an increasingly important public force and the revivalist spirit grew. In 1830, however, the congregation split when a group of independent-thinking parishioners, resenting the strong methods of Dr. Wisner, organized a Protestant Reformed Dutch Church. As the schismatics left (Simeon DeWitt among them), they were given letters in good standing from the Presbyterian Church; the first two contributions to the new church's building fund came from two Presbyterian elders. The breakaway group built a Greek Revival structure on the corner of Seneca and Geneva streets, which was replaced in 1884 by the present church building (now St. Catherine Greek Orthodox Church). In 1872 this congregation, apparently still independent in thought, decided to sever its connection with the Reformed Church and after some legal controversy formed as an independent Congregational Church. The present First Congregational Church left its downtown building in 1969 and has been located on Highland Road in Cayuga Heights ever since.

Meanwhile, Dr. Wisner resigned his post with the Presbyterian congregation in 1831, which by then had more than 800 members. He returned in 1838, however, and was reinstalled, and by 1842 the congregation had received 1,349 members. The church building was replaced in 1853 by a Gothic structure and again in 1900 by the present Romanesque building, with stained-glass windows in the western apse.

The Methodists founded their society in Ithaca in 1817. Two Methodist congregations coexisted in Ithaca from 1851, until they came together to form St. Paul's United Methodist Church in 1960. The present church building dating from 1907 stands on the site of the original church, which had been built in 1820 at a cost of $5,000 on the northwest corner of Aurora and Mill (Court) streets; the lot had been donated by Simeon DeWitt. The church was noted for having the first church bell in the village and was replaced by a brick structure on the same site in 1866.

St. John's Episcopal Church was organized in 1822 and held sporadic services in a small, plain, brick church built in 1824 on the southwest corner of Seneca and Cayuga streets. In 1860 the present Gothic church was completed. Other early church organizations included the Lutherans, and the Quakers, long active in the Jacksonville area. The Baptists built a brick church on their present site in DeWitt Park in 1831 (the present Romanesque-style church was designed by William Henry Miller and put up in 1890). The Roman Catholics organized in 1830 and established the Ithaca parish in 1848. Catholics in Trumansburg bought the old Methodist Church and rededicated it in 1857; before that time it was not uncommon for men to walk to and from Ithaca to attend Mass. The Immaculate Conception Church in Ithaca dates from 1896, and St. Catherine of Siena in the northeast section from 1960. The First Unitarian Society came later, founded by Ezra Cornell and others in 1865; their present Romanesque church building in Ithaca was designed by William Henry Miller.

A Jewish congregation was organized in 1906 and several years later an orthodox congregation was formed. In 1924 the two groups joined forces with the Hillel Foundation Chapter at Cornell University. Temple Beth-El was constructed in 1928 on the corner of Court and Tioga streets in Ithaca and remains today the only Jewish temple in the county.

The St. James African Methodist Episcopal Zion Church at 116 Cleveland Avenue (formerly Wheat Street) in downtown Ithaca (figure 66), constructed in 1836 and recently restored, has played an important role in black history and—with Calvary Baptist Church—in black culture, with special music programs, revivals, and celebrations. From the early days of its existence the church was Ithaca's chief station on the Underground Railroad. Tompkins County served as a significant link in this well-organized system, and although information is sparse (the system being illegal, people did not talk about it, much less leave records), we do know that many black fugitives after escaping slavery in the South moved through the county or settled here (at least until the enactment of the Fugitive Slave Law in 1850).

In the 1840s (the greatest traffic was between 1850 and 1860) a network of stations was established between several southern

Institutions, Organizations, Agencies

66. St. James African Methodist Episcopal Zion Church. Shown at the turn of the century, this church was restored on the exterior in 1981. Originally a one-story building, it was enlarged over the years. Its bell was a gift of the Ithaca community in 1887.

States—especially Virginia, Maryland, and Delaware (through which the Mason-Dixon Line ran)—and free states to the north, particularly those bordering Canada. Black churches in the north provided safe haven for the fugitives; often the pastors were escaped slaves themselves. Almost every pastor of St. James Church during this period was a stationmaster on the railroad. Other religious groups helped as well, especially the Quakers. Three major routes led from the south, well charted and secret; the one affecting Tompkins County came up the Susquehanna valley to the principal stopping place of Elmira. There it split, with one branch going north and west, the other coming through Ithaca. Most of the fugitives came from the Elmira main stop by foot, wagon, or coaches. In Tompkins County about a dozen communities had stations on the routes. The main station was Ithaca and aside from St. James Church, which housed runaways in the basement (many brought there by Harriet Tubman, who made at least nineteen trips south between 1840 and 1861 to free her people and who was a frequent worshiper at the church), several private homes served as shelters. It is known that Francis Bloodgood started harboring runaways in the attic of his house at 326 South Cayuga Street as early as 1820; the house was purchased in 1824 by Titus Brum, who used a secret room with a trap door over an old bake oven for the same purpose. Other known hiding places were at 126 East State Street (formerly the Brooks Block) and at 214 West State. Fugitives were hidden as well on the steamboat *Simeon DeWitt*, which provided transportation on one of the routes north, via the lake to Cayuga Bridge and Auburn. Other routes were by land through Ludlowville and Lansing, through Etna and Peruville, and on the west shore through Jacksonville and Trumansburg.

One prominent leader in the organization was George A. Johnson, a Free Negro, an active member of the Republican party, and a well-known Ithaca barber. He could call on his lawyer friend Ben Johnson and on other white Ithacans for help; he provided food, clothing, money, places on the steamboat, and other needed services. He also used his skills in a particularly practical way, by shaving beards and changing hair styles. In the 1840s and 1850s he was successful in sending more than 110 individuals on to safety in the north.

Institutions, Organizations, Agencies

After staying in various safe places in and near Ithaca (the Danby farm of Lewis Beers harbored runaways in the barn, for example), the fugitives moved to stops on the way north: the Hayt Church, the Farmer's Inn in Jacksonville (where proprietor Horace Cooper provided food, clothing, and shelter), two houses in Etna on the Lower Creek Road (one at #118 has a secret circular room under the kitchen floor with two trap doors), Ludlowville where stationmaster Benjamin Joy (of temperance movement fame) took care of them. Some fugitives stayed in the county, but the Fugitive Slave Law (part of the compromise that admitted California to the Union as a free state) made it exceedingly dangerous to remain. It also made things increasingly dangerous for those participating in the underground operation. The new law required northern states to aid southern states in getting slaves back and legally sanctioned the sending of slave catchers north to apprehend runaways. But the railroad kept on going and successfully offered refuge, aid, and safe passage to several thousand black slaves. It was a splendid example of well-organized community cooperation in assistance to others and courageous dedication to the ideals of freedom.

[5]

Recreation and Cultural Activities

EARLY travelers through Tompkins County, struck by the unusual beauty of our region, recounted their impressions of the large waterfalls, the steep and craggy gorges, the grand views, the fine woods.[21] One popular story has the Cornell professor standing on the suspension bridge over Fall Creek late one afternoon gazing at the gorge and the valley below; when asked by a colleague what he is doing, he replies, "oh, I'm enjoying my fringe benefits." Indeed he is not alone. The scenery clearly is one of the county's assets and enjoying it a perennial pastime of both residents and the many visitors who have come over the years to look at the beauty of our surroundings (figure 67). Tourism has always been a leading business of the county. And even if we put aside the extraordinary landscape, our region has provided through the years many opportunities for recreation, pastimes for every taste.

Tompkins County—perhaps because of its concentration of schools and colleges—has an unusual collection of musical groups, art galleries, and theaters, not to mention an enormous number of creative individuals. The Tompkins County Arts Council has a listing of more than fifty member organizations, representing hundreds, even thousands of people with an unusual interest in and enthusiastic dedication to the arts. Even back in the early days, when recreation and cultural pursuits were not nearly so important as today, the settlers made serious efforts to beautify

Recreation and Cultural Activities

67. Ithaca Falls. This picture, taken in March 1936, provides a view frequently seen after heavy spring rains. Cornell University's buildings are to the right and the Stewart Avenue bridge in the center. In the lower right can be seen the waterway created by Ezra Cornell's tunnel.

their surroundings, to develop their creativity, and to enjoy what leisure they had. By the early 1820s groups had formed for debating, the promotion of drama, and reading.

Parks and Forests

Municipal parks. The earliest park in the county was DeWitt Park in the center of Ithaca. When Simeon DeWitt laid out Ithaca in the early 1800s, he set aside the area as the village green. DeWitt owned much of the downtown land in Ithaca and designated some of it for special uses in his plan. Several lots around the green were set aside for private homes, and he sold about half of the park area in the late 1810s to the Presbyterian Church, which actually established the first park on the land. The church later acquired the rest of the park land in an exchange with DeWitt. The park came to be known as the Publick Square, its name being changed to DeWitt Park some time after Simeon DeWitt's death in 1834. According to the original deed, the land was to be maintained as a public walk and promenade. One report from the 1820s notes the absence of sidewalks and cows grazing right up to the church door; at night the faithful needed a lantern to avoid cow "cushions."[22] In 1856 church and village reached an agreement specifying that the church would retain title to the land while the village would care for and control the park; this agreement is still in force. Between about 1910 and 1960 DeWitt Park served as a campus for the Ithaca Conservatory of Music, which became Ithaca College in 1931. Between the Boardman House, which was the administration building, and the Baptist Church the conservatory built several buildings (only one is still standing and houses the Board of Elections). Also in the park area stand the Presbyterian Church and the First Baptist Church, the latter built of limestone in 1890. The area around the park has been designated as both a local and a national historical district. Two band pavilions were built in the park in the 1860s (figure 68), and more recently the park has been used for an Art in the Park show in May, where the work of local and regional artists is displayed and sold, and for the Wednesday morning Farmers' Market during the summer along the Buffalo and Cayuga street sidewalks.

The common in Dryden was established around 1820 with a gift of land by Abram Griswold to the people of Dryden, "six rods square" on each of the four corners, designating it as public land. All but the northeast corner were later built on, and in the 1850s the common land was redeeded to the Presbyterian Church. The common today is located between the Presbyterian and Methodist churches; in earlier days it had a bandstand and an ornate fountain. Dryden also has two other recreational areas: Montgomery Park on Elm Street, with tennis courts that are

Recreation and Cultural Activities

68. Bandstand in Ithaca's DeWitt Park (c. 1865). In the background is the Gothic Presbyterian Church, built in 1853 and replaced in 1900 by the present church building. This photograph is by Joseph C. Burritt, a gifted local photographer who died in 1889 (see also figure 92).

flooded in winter for ice skating and a new bandstand built in 1976, and Dryden Lake, an old Indian hunting and fishing area used today for skating parties and picnicking.

Communities all over the county have small parks and recreational areas; every public school has its playing fields and playground. The Town of Lansing Park at Myers Point was developed in the 1970s with play areas, picnic facilities, and a marina.

The city of Ithaca has several small parks—among them Washington Park downtown, about two acres developed in 1908; the Van Natta's Dam site and trail, of special interest to wildflower and bird lovers; and the Wood Street Park, with playing fields for baseball and softball. Under the auspices of Cornell University are the Laboratory of Ornithology at Sapsucker Woods, a bird sanctuary with 180 acres of undisturbed habitat and trails and a main building with exhibits, brochures, a bookstore, and an observatory; Cornell Plantations on 2,600 acres, with trails, botanical gardens, an arboretum, woodlands, and wildflowers; and Arnot Forest in the southwest corner of the county, with nine miles of foot trails. The city of Ithaca possesses and maintains the two large developed recreational areas, both located at the head of Cayuga Lake: Stewart Park, privately owned and operated in the late nineteenth century as an amusement park under the name Renwick Park and later expanded in the 1920s, and the more recent Cass Park, developed in the early 1970s. Both have played a role in the history of Tompkins County.

The Renwick Tract was a square mile of land that Andrew Moody (or Moodie) drew by lot in 1790. Moody sold it later that year to James Renwick and he in turn passed it on to his son William. William died in 1808 leaving the property to his wife and seven children, the youngest being Robert Jeffrey Renwick, known around Ithaca as Major Renwick. In 1820 the major took possession of the property, a 640-acre tract along the east shore of the lake. The greater part of the area remained undeveloped for over one hundred years; it included what would become areas of Stewart Park, the Remington Salt Works site, Renwick Heights, Cayuga Heights, part of Cornell Heights, and Lakeview Cemetery. Along the lakeshore ran a long series of sand bars, and before the development of the park the area was a favorite place for horse racing.

After the owners of the Ithaca Street Railway, engineer Herman Bergholtz and financier Horace Hand, gained control of the railway and electric light companies in 1891, they extended the street railway line to Railroad Avenue (the present Lincoln Street is the northern part of Railroad Avenue, which curved around to about Buffalo Street in the West End, along the railroad tracks, and on a path very close to the present Route 13 bypass). The owners incorporated the Cayuga Lake Railroad Company, which then purchased the lakeshore property from the James Renwick estate. In the summer of 1894 the company built a railroad line from Railroad Avenue to the lake and developed forty acres of land at the terminus as Renwick Park. James Jeffrey Renwick, great-grandson of the James Renwick who had bought the land in 1790, was the first superintendent of the gardens. Renwick Park was an amusement park, with lawns, woods, and paths; it had a long boat pier, vaudeville theater, zoo, pavilion, casino, ice cream parlor, and bathhouse (figure 69). Pat Conway's band gave concerts during the summer months and the various entertainments attracted many visitors to the park, often on excursions. Sometime after the turn of the century, however, such amusement parks went out of vogue, and the facilities were closed down. In 1914 the park was leased to the Wharton Studios for the filming of movies and was the scene of many silent films of the era.

While Edwin C. Stewart (son of Mayor David B. Stewart) was mayor in 1921, the city purchased the park for $30,000; Edwin died in office, leaving in his will $150,000 for the development of the park, which bears his name. Herman Bergholtz, early owner and developer of the park who was to become mayor of Ithaca himself ten years later, was given the job of restoring the badly neglected facility, which was run down and cluttered with movie shacks and dilapidated sets. The city park also incorporated two other parcels of land lying east of the Inlet, which had been conveyed to the city in 1910; one had been put aside as a bird sanctuary, the other and much larger piece was developed as the municipal golf course in 1935 and named the Newman Golf Course for Jared T. Newman, a former mayor of Ithaca who had leased most of the land. At the same time that the golf course was being built, in part with funds of the Works Progress Administration, large areas of Stewart Park were filled in and raised about three feet. (In those days hitting a ball to the outfield had often meant losing it in the swamp.) Most of the detailed plans for the park were carried out, though a projected bridge to connect the golf course with the old airport across the Inlet never materialized. The 195-acre site is now one of the county's principal recreational

69. Renwick Park, Ithaca. In its heyday during the late nineteenth century the park had crowds of people, many parasols, and heavy horse-and-buggy traffic. And the band played on. In the background is the steamboat pier. See also figure 73.

areas, with extended lakeshore, playing fields, zoo, duck pen, tennis courts, a bike route, a playground, and boat rentals.

The land that was developed into Cass Park came to the city in several different parcels. One area was acquired in 1925 as part of lands put in trust for the city by former mayor Newman and others. The city had purchased another area, between the Inlet and the lakefront, in 1908 and along with other lands originally earmarked it as a municipal lakefront park. When the Inlet was dredged for the Barge Canal in the early 1900s, the marshland to the west had been filled in and planted with peach trees. They didn't grow, and the orchard eventually became a flying field. This area was leased to the Thomas-Morse Aviation Company for the testing of airplanes and for an aviation school before, during, and after World War I. Eventually the land (about 122 acres) was developed and used as a municipal airport (the third-oldest airport in the United States, with a large hangar and a seaplane landing site on the Inlet) until the present Tompkins County Airport was built after World War II. In 1929 the city bought yet another area, several small pieces of property between the railroad tracks and the Inlet called the Silent City (see figure 61), a collection of shacks put up in the late nineteenth century and later abandoned. The shacks were removed as part of the park project. The last parcel to be acquired by the city was farther west and owned by the Lehigh Valley Railroad; the land, including the old railroad loop, passed to the city in 1966. A city marina was built, but in the early 1970s the state took over that area and constructed a state marina at about the same time that Cass Park was being developed. A few years previously the flood control channel was dug; work on that project had started in 1968 and was completed the following year. The earth dredged from the channel was used to fill the area that is today the southern portion of Cass Park. Development of Cass Park continued through 1971 and 1972. The new Route 89 was finished through the park and is called Park Road; part of it is built on a segment of the old railroad loop. Plans for a bridge across the flood control channel from the end of the old Taughannock Boulevard to the new Park Road were put on hold to await the proposed development of Route 96; a dozen years later they are still waiting.

The ice rink at Cass Park was opened in November 1972, followed in the summer of 1973 by an olympic-size swimming pool and ball fields. More playing fields have since been added (there are twenty today, of which four are lit) as well as a minipool and a pavilion built by the Kiwanis Club. The park, which also has tennis courts and a pedestrian path to the city along the Inlet, is used year round. The northern area of the park houses the Allan H. Treman State Marine Park and the old hangar. The city leases the building and adjacent parking area to the Hangar Theatre, which has renovated and converted the hangar into a modern theater used during the summer.

State parks. Tompkins County has considerable land designated as state forest—the Connecticut Hill Wildlife Management Area in the towns of Newfield and Enfield, Danby State Forest in the town of Danby, the Shindagin, Potato Hill, and Robinson Hollow state forests in the town of Caroline, and the Yellow Barn and Hammond Hill state forests in Dryden. A small area near the county's eastern border north of Speedsville has also been reforested by the county.

The Finger Lakes region has seventeen state parks, of which four are grouped close together in Tompkins County. In addition the headquarters of the Finger Lakes Park Commission are situated on the hillside between the upper and lower entrances of Taughannock Falls State Park in the town of Ulysses. A state park plan was implemented in 1924 with the establishment of a park system based on regions with unpaid regional park commissioners. The State Council of Parks had its first meeting in 1924, and the Finger Lakes Parks Commission was created in April of that year. There are seven commissioners; the commission is charged with preserving the reservations, parks, and parkways in a natural form, while keeping them as safe as possible for the public. Instrumental in the development of the parks of our region were two Ithaca residents—Robert H. Treman and his son, Allan H. Treman—who served as chairmen of the commission and donated time and considerable property to the park system. Under the jurisdiction of the commission are four parks, Enfield Glen, Buttermilk Falls, Taughannock Falls, and the Treman marina.

Enfield Glen has been open since 1920 and was donated by Mr. and Mrs. Robert H. Treman; in 1937 the original name of the park was changed to the Robert H. Treman State Park. The park has grown from an original 387 acres in 1920 to the present 1,020. The gorge is considered by many to be the most beautiful of the region (figure 1), with a 115-foot waterfall and stunning views of the surrounding landscape. The old mill at the upper entrance was built by Jared Treman in 1838 (according to the most reliable sources) on the site of the original gristmill, which was part of a small settlement and which burned down. Used for grinding grain, it was known as a turbine mill, that is, the wheel was horizontal, and the water was diverted by two sluiceways, both of which were washed away in the flood of 1935. The mill was used as a park pavilion for many years until it was put on the National Register of Historic Places in the late 1970s (figures 24 and 25). Most of the old mill is intact, including the king wheel, elevators, and some machinery, and is open to visitors between mid-May and mid-October. In 1984 the mill was reroofed and repainted in two-tone grey.

Buttermilk Falls was opened to the public in 1924 and today has an area of 605 acres (figure 70). The land with the glen proper was given in 1924 by Mr. and Mrs. Robert H. Treman. Within the park are ten waterfalls and an artificial lake created with the building of Scott Dam in 1875. This lake, now named the Robert H. Treman Lake, served as a reservoir for the city's water supply until 1903.

The first portion of Taughannock Falls State Park, an area of 64 acres, was purchased by the state in 1924; it has since been enlarged to 742 acres. The Robert H. Tremans leased additional property, including the southern half of the main falls, to the county in 1912, and the commission subsequently acquired this land. The 215-foot falls (called The Great Falls in the Woods by the Indian settlers) are one of the outstanding natural attractions of the northeastern United States and have drawn many visitors through the years (figure 71).

Both the Treman and Taughannock parks were extensively damaged in the July 1935 flood. During the 1930s the Civilian Conservation Corps (part of President Roosevelt's New Deal) was organized to put the city youth to work on the nation's resources. In 1935 there were four CCC camps in the county, and the campers did extensive work in the three state parks, including building the stone steps on the north trail and the cabins at the lower end of Treman. At the time of the flood they did considerable rescue and clean-up work. All three parks have swimming and camping facilities, as well as picnic areas and playgrounds.

70. Buttermilk Falls State Park. Pinnacle Rock in this gorge is one of many striking rock formations that are part of the county's unusual scenery.

Recreation and Cultural Activities

71. Taughannock Falls, Taughannock Falls State Park.

The Allan H. Treman State Marine Park, located adjacent to the developed area of Ithaca's municipal Cass Park, is the largest inland marina in New York State, with 399 berths.

Pastimes and Events

The early residents of Tompkins County had few opportunities for recreation, and it is not until the second half of the nineteenth century that one begins to read accounts of leisure time activities. There were the traditional family pastimes and travel. There

72. Parade on State Street. This parade was one of many held in Ithaca in the 1890s and early 1900s as part of the annual Central New York Firemen's Convention.

were parades (figures 13 and 72) and the circus, which in those days advertised—besides the usual rare animals and strong men—"scenic" riders, jugglers, and a "great ballet troupe." But recreation was limited in a society that put emphasis on hard work. With the abundance of athletic activity and sporting events we have today, it is rather hard to believe that Andrew Dickson White would write in his *Autobiography*: "one of the best investments I ever made was in giving a racing-boat to the Cornell crew on Cayuga Lake."[23]

Boat and train excursions. During the nineteenth century travel was probably the most important leisure activity. With the completion of the Erie Canal and the stagecoach and boat combination, which rather quickly became the train and boat combination, people started to get around a good deal. Steamboat trips on the lake were very popular in the 1830s and 1840s. Passengers could

73. Cayuga Lake Steamers at Renwick Pier. This photograph, dating from around 1905, shows the *Iroquois* on the left, with the *Frontenac* behind and the *Mohawk* to the right.

take the *DeWitt Clinton* which departed on a daily trip from Ithaca to Cayuga Bridge and back. One account of the trip calls it "one of the most delightful water excursions to be enjoyed in any part of our country."[24]

The 1880s opened an era of great prosperity, and various amusements became widespread. The railroads and boat companies planned special excursions—the Cayuga Lake Railroad, for example, would take passengers from the south and east up to a favorite resort, Atwaters, on the east shore of the lake. Taughannock Landing, north of Lansing, was a stop on the line, and from there tourists could take the steamboat to see the falls on the other side. The lake pleasure boats (figures 73 and 74) enjoyed great popularity, and up and down the lakeshore were boat landings and the accompaniments of a busy summer resort. At the Trumansburg Landing, for example, were a hotel, a dance pavilion, and boat rentals, as well as camping facilities and cottages. Grand hotels with such names as Wind & Wave, Glenwood,

74. The Steamboat *Frontenac*. The most famous of the Cayuga Lake steamers made her maiden voyage on June 4, 1870. The landing was located where Cascadilla Creek joined the Inlet.

Frontenac Beach Hotel, Sheldrake House, and Cayuga Lake Hotel played host to the crowds who arrived by lake boat. Excursions were planned, stopping at various docks along the lake, and the amusement park at the head of Cayuga Lake was designed in part to accommodate the tourists who arrived at the Renwick Park steamboat pier (see figures 69 and 73). There was band music and dancing and good food, with some theater vaudeville mixed in for good measure. Fashions eventually changed, however, and business slackened, virtually ending after the flagship of the fleet, the *Frontenac* (figures 73 and 74), burned at Long Point in 1907; only a few, much smaller pleasure boats stayed in operation.

Recreation and Cultural Activities

75. Prize-Winning Baby. This young winner doesn't look any too pleased about the pretty baby prize (given for years by the *Ithaca News,* a daily paper purchased by Gannett in 1919 and merged with the *Ithaca Journal*). Note the hats and the elaborate wicker pram with parasol.

Another popular excursion in the early 1900s was worked out by Colonel J. V. McIntyre of Rogues Harbor (figure 30). He had the idea of running a half-mile railroad link between the South Lansing depot and the hotel, and for a time it made six trips a day, thus providing Ithacans with a pleasant outing, easily accessible and close to home.

Fairs and festivals. The county has had its share of fairs and festivals, and the tradition continues today. The fairs have always been a part of the strong agricultural interests of the region. Tompkins County had its first agricultural exhibition at the Ithaca Hotel in 1820, the year the Tompkins County Agricultural Society was founded. This group was reorganized several times, and in 1858 Ezra Cornell served as its president. The fairs started in 1839, and in 1855 the society purchased land near the steamboat landing and on this tract put up a two-story exhibition hall and laid out a trotting track. In 1875 this property was sold, and a 45-acre site was purchased in the southwest part of the village on which were erected buildings for floral exhibits and for the judging of farm animals and produce, as well as a half-mile trotting course (see figures 6 and 11). For the first time in 1875 a prize was given out to the handsomest baby shown at the fair, a custom that continued for many years (figure 75). The Dryden Agricultural Society was organized in 1856, with permanent fair grounds on East Main Street. The Dryden Fair for a while was considered the largest in the state; the last event was held in 1917 and the fair building, a twelve-sided structure (figure 21), was torn down in 1953. Today Dryden has an annual festival in October. The Trumansburg Fair has been held annually in July for more than one hundred years and until recently was well known for its racing events. More recent annual events are the Ellis Hollow Fair, which started in 1953 and takes place the first Saturday in September and the Brooktondale Apple Festival, which follows in October. Newfield has its Old Home Weekend & Empire Farm Days and Groton too celebrates its Old Home Days in August every year. Also each August Ithaca plays host to the Upstate Craft Fair: for three days the fair provides exhibits and demonstrations by craft people from all over the state.

Sports. Since the turn of the century spectator and participatory sports have been very popular in Tompkins County. Cornell University and Ithaca College have offered sporting events of all kinds to watch, as have the public schools. Football and hockey games have long been popular and in the 1930s crew races could be watched from observation trains that ran along the lakeshore. For years the annual Heptagonals, indoor athletic events with participants from Ivy League institutions and the two eastern service academies, took place each February in Cornell's Barton Hall; their location now rotates. Tompkins County played host to the U.S. Junior Olympics in 1974 and to the Drum Corps International Championships in 1975. Every year on or close to the Fourth of

Recreation and Cultural Activities

76. Cornell Mud Rush. This competition between freshmen and sophomores was held every spring in the early 1900s. It was abandoned in 1926.

July there is a fireworks show in Cornell's Schoellkopf Field, with marching bands and ground displays.

Tompkins County has also hosted some fairly unusual sports during this century. From the early 1900s through 1926 the coming of spring was marked by the annual "mud rush," which would have to be seen to be believed (figure 76). Today architecture students construct and then burn a green dragon. There was bobsledding on the Buffalo Street hill, on nights when conditions were good, until a fatal accident at the corner of Buffalo and Aurora streets ended it. In 1898 a dam was built across Fall Creek forming Beebe Lake. For many years a toboggan slide shot sleds out on the lake (figure 77), and until recent times many people enjoyed ice skating in the winter there and boating (especially canoeing) in the summer. April now sees the annual Fall Creek White Water Derby, starting in Etna and ending in Varna.

77. Toboggan Run on Cornell's Beebe Lake. Located on the south side of the lake, the toboggan slide, shown here around 1900, was very popular for years. There were two successive trestles for the run, one of wood (seen here), the other of steel, made by the Groton Bridge Company.

Organizations in Recreation and the Arts

A leading recreational and social service organization of the area is the YMCA, which started life as a gathering place for young men and has since grown to a large facility serving the entire county. The first meeting of the local Y was held in 1868 in the reading room of the Cornell Public Library; a letter from 1872 reports that the Y "used among the students and the University has fixed up a very fine room for them in the College and have furnished it for them . . . and the Ministers from the Town meet with them at their Meetings."[25] The organization then faded away to be revived between the years 1889 and 1907 when it offered evening educational classes, lectures, and religious meetings in quarters secured in a building on the corner of Seneca and Tioga streets, with a gym and showers. The Y then moved to the Titus Block on West State Street (figure 88); in 1907 it bought a lot on the corner of Buffalo and Tioga streets, where a new building was erected (figure

Recreation and Cultural Activities

93). The project was aided by a gift from George Williams, the same man who had chaired the Y's first meeting in 1868, and the new building was dedicated in 1908. The YMCA then became a local pioneer in physical education and recreation, offering through the years programs that were expanded to include first young women, then children, then adults. It was especially noted for its swimming instruction and camping programs. The Y building burned down in 1978 and has been replaced by a large modern facility opened in 1984 on the south side of Lansing Village.

In the early days the most important settlements had some sort of farmers' organization, usually the Grange, a national society devoted to the commercial and fellowship interests of farmers (the first grange in the state was formed at Fredonia in 1867, and the first in Tompkins County was Pioneer Grange 230, organized in Danby in 1874). Today several towns have local community centers. The Women's Community Building, the Southside Center, and the Greater Ithaca Activities Center (located in the former Central elementary school), the Ellis Hollow Community Center (dating from 1953), the recently organized Cayuga Heights Community Center (it too has headquarters in a former school) all are part of a growing movement of community organization with educational and recreational programs. The Senior Citizens Center on South Geneva Street is headquarters for activities for Tompkins County's retired citizens; along with similar centers in other towns, it offers services for the elderly and such activities as lectures, trips, and opportunities for work, both paid and volunteer.

Many clubs with a cultural orientation have existed in the county, some for many years (figure 78). Founded in the last century, for example, the old Town & Gown Club on Stewart Avenue enjoyed great popularity. The Cornell University Campus Club has also been in operation since the end of the nineteenth century, and today it offers (for women with a university connection mainly) activities that range from cross-country skiing and gourmet cooking to play reading and musical performance. The Savage Club of Ithaca was established at the end of the nineteenth century thanks to British historian Henry Morse Stephens. He had been appointed to the Cornell faculty by Andrew Dickson White in the year 1894 and introduced the visiting Cornell Glee Club to the

78. Ithaca Choral Club. One forerunner of the Cornell Savoyards was this group, shown in May 1893, the principals for Gilbert and Sullivan's *Pirates of Penzance*. The two men to the right in the top row are Robert H. Treman and Hollis Dann (see figure 81).

Savage Club of London in 1895. The Ithaca club, formed in tribute to the hospitality of the London club, has over forty members and gathers musical and dramatic talent to present an annual show each spring.

The Tompkins County Arts Council was established in the late 1970s to provide service and assistance to Tompkins County artists and arts organizations. It currently has fifty-three member groups, among them local businesses interested in promoting the arts, galleries, schools, musical and theatrical groups, museums, and community centers. The council provides funding guidance for the community and serves as a clearinghouse for information on research, publication, and promotion of artistic works and material. The arts have played an important role in the development of the county, especially in Ithaca. In particular it was the late nineteenth

Recreation and Cultural Activities

century, with its burst of prosperity and increase of leisure activity, that saw the appearance of a number of theaters and buildings devoted to the arts.

Theaters. Ezra Cornell, in founding the Cornell Public Library, made provision for a large meeting room to furnish space for musical and dramatic productions as well as lectures and official university gatherings. The third floor of the Clinton Hall (figure 87), built between 1847 and 1851 next door to the Clinton House, was a large room that served during the second half of the nineteenth century as a public meeting hall and entertainment center. The hall, with allegorical paintings on the ceiling, seated five hundred people; it was used for political meetings as well as for exhibits, some of which were luridly patriotic displays. It had drop scenery for these exhibits which depicted the Siege of Monterey and for the vaudeville performances and shows put on by traveling companies. The hall was also used for dance classes and, later, for movies. At the time of this writing it faces demolition.

The Wilgus Block was built in 1868, and the Wilgus Opera House occupied its third and fourth floors with an auditorium seating 1,600 people (figures 9 and 81). For years it served as Ithaca's main entertainment center, and the young Cornell Glee Club, which began with the new university and was formally organized in 1875, sang three choral pieces in a "Grand Concert" held there in April 1876. Between 1894 and 1911 part of the opera house was used by the Ithaca Conservatory of Music.

The Lyceum Theater was built on South Cayuga Street in 1893 at a cost of about $35,000 and became the city's main theater. It was an L-shaped building with the entrance on Cayuga Street and the auditorium roughly on the site of Ithaca's present city offices, that is, it ran behind the buildings facing west on Cayuga Street. In use for about thirty years, the theater was considered by many to be the greatest cultural institution in the county. With seating for 1,200, it had four private boxes, nineteen loges, and a 60 × 40 foot stage (figure 79). The leading traveling companies came to perform, and nearly every famous actor and actress in America played their greatest roles there. One could have seen Otis Skinner and Sir Johnston Forbes-Robertson among others, as well as the great

79. Lyceum Theater, Ithaca. Despite hard wooden benches for seats, the theater had a sumptuous and elaborate decor, with the drop curtain representing the Port of Leghorn.

Sarah Bernhardt who in 1916 played in three one-act French plays. One-night traveling performances later went out of favor; the theater was subsequently used for movies before being torn down in 1934. Since then Ithaca has had other theaters, mostly for movies—the Star Theater, built in 1911, was located across from the present Tompkins County Trust Company buildings on Seneca Street, and was later used by Ithaca College for physical education. The Crescent Theater on North Aurora Street was built in 1916 and is Ithaca's oldest surviving movie palace. It later became a dance hall, and it too was used by Ithaca College for a gym; it became a nightclub in 1976 and houses offices today. In 1914 or thereabouts Ithacans could see a two-hour show three times every weekday at the Star; the program included one hour of movies (some made in Ithaca, the theater being the trial house for Wharton Studio films), and one hour of three acts of vaudeville, all for the

Recreation and Cultural Activities

price of 15 cents. (At that time an outing at Renwick—now Stewart—Park cost 5 cents carfare each way.)

The Strand Theatre was built in 1917, a completely local project and constructed by the Driscoll Lumber Company, mainly to house traveling theatrical groups but also as a movie house. Famous actors and actresses appeared there too, including Helen Hayes, George M. Cohan, and Katherine Cornell. In the 1950s the Strand became exclusively a movie house and it was closed in 1975. Despite the efforts of local backers, who reopened the theater and renovated the interior, and despite performances there by imported and local jazz and rock groups, the Ballet Guild of Ithaca, and the Ithaca Opera Association, the theater was closed again in 1982. It faces a very uncertain future. The State Theater on West State Street presented vaudeville and other stage shows as well as movies in the 1930s and 1940s; when it originally opened in 1928 (in a building constructed in 1915 as an automobile showroom and garage), it was billed as Ithaca's first "semi-atmospheric" theater and seated 1,818 people. In 1976, with the enclosure of the balcony, it was converted into two small theaters.

Ithaca's stages today include the Hangar Theatre in Cass Park which seats about 360 people. The present theatrical organization, which has gone through several transformations, put on its first full production in 1975 and presents a summer season that combines local amateur and professional talent with visiting professional actors and production personnel. The Hangar also sponsors a theater program called the Younger Generation and has recently been producing short experimental plays as a prelude to the main show. Central Casting Theater, a group organized in the late 1970s, presents plays all year round from the modern repertory. They started out in a former body shop (first auto, then human) and in 1984 renovated a portion of the interior of the Masonic Temple, creating a 140-seat theater. The First Street Playhouse, a very small U-shaped theater that seats only about thirty, mostly produces work by local writers (one of whom is a teenage musician and playwright) and involves people of all ages in its productions. Both Cornell and Ithaca College present plays during the school year, at theaters in Willard Straight Hall and the Dillingham Performing Arts Center respectively. Cornell University also hosts the Cornell Savoyards, a group that has been performing two Gilbert and Sullivan shows each year since the late 1950s. And in Dryden the Dryden Footlighters produce several shows per year.

Trumansburg built its Opera Block in 1871; the Opera House occupied the third floor of the building (figure 37). From then until 1922, when the entire block burned to the ground, the Opera House was a place for local meetings and offered various entertainments—a sampling includes an Italian opera troupe, a lecture by Horace Greeley on "toil," theatrical troupes, the Trumansburg Praying Band with its lady evangelist, and magicians, as well as church festivals, local dances (often with the Lyceum Orchestra of Ithaca), and suppers. In 1893 the Dryden Opera House was built with an auditorium seating 500 to 600 people. It opened on January 1, 1894, with a dramatic production and for many years offered plays, musical and minstrel shows, and band concerts. Interest fell off in the 1920s although the Opera House was used as a public entertainment center until the 1930s. It burned in 1963.

Musical groups. Special music organizations continue to provide entertainment for the county. The university and the colleges provide concert series and recitals by faculty and visiting musicians. The Ithaca Opera Association, founded in 1949, has put on two major productions each year since that time. The association has recently expanded its activities to include opera workshops and educational programs. The Cayuga Chamber Orchestra dates from 1976 and is made up of professional musicians who live, teach, study, and perform in Ithaca and neighboring communities. From 1977 to 1984 the orchestra's music director and conductor was Karel Husa, an internationally known composer and winner of a Pulitzer prize.

Over the years Tompkins County's band tradition has been very strong. Toward the end of the nineteenth century and well into the twentieth, band music enjoyed enormous popularity; it was an important element in the park scene. DeWitt Park had a bandstand, as did the park in Dryden, and the Renwick amusement park put on band concerts as a regular part of its entertainment (figures 68 and 69). The town of Lansing had its cornet band (figure 31), as did

Recreation and Cultural Activities

Dryden, and numerous old photographs from the turn of the century show different groups in uniform, ready to get out and play. There were marching bands, and there were concert bands, and there was "Patsy" Conway. In the opening section of his popular song, "76 Trombones" (from the hit musical *The Music Man*), Meredith Willson has his protagonist describe the scene created by a wonderful combination of bands: ". . . and you feel something akin to the electric thrill I once enjoyed when Gilmore, Liberatti, Pat Conway, the great Creatore, W. C. Handy, and John Philip Sousa all came to town on the very same historic day." In that list of famous band leaders is Patrick Conway, who studied at the Ithaca Conservatory and in 1894 became the conductor of the Cornell Band. He also played in the Lyceum Theater Orchestra, which performed in the theater but also all around the county.

Over the next thirteen years Conway organized the Ithaca Town Band, also known as Pat Conway's Band (figure 80). It had some wonderful musicians, among them members of the New York Philharmonic who came on their summer break to play with the group. One player undoubtedly spoke for many when he said "Conway is the best man I ever worked for."[26] In 1908 Pat Conway took his band to the San Francisco Exposition, and that same year he moved to Syracuse. He returned to Ithaca in 1922, however, to become the director of the Ithaca School of Band Instruments, one of the schools affiliated with the Ithaca Conservatory of Music. During those last years he ran the band school and directed the activities of the Conway Band, which played concerts at the pavilion in Stewart Park, among many other engagements, and made recordings.

The presence of Pat Conway on the Ithaca scene had its lasting effect, for the Ithaca Conservatory of Music became Ithaca College in 1931; several decades later the college took over the Conway Band and its Department of Music under Walter Beeler (who had gone to the Conway band school) grew to be one of the best in the country. For many years the Ithaca College concert band had a nationwide reputation, and the college provided outstanding training for band players and conductors. Ithaca College today has two different bands, and Cornell University has the Cornell Concert Band, which plays several performances a year, including a popu-

80. The Ithaca Band (1903). Pat Conway stands behind the bass drum.

lar outdoor concert on Libe Slope, the hill west of the Cornell libraries, and the Big Red Marching Band of over one hundred players. We also have a community band, the Ithaca Concert Band, founded in the mid-1970s and since 1977 under the direction of Henry Neubert, who is on the music faculty at Ithaca College. This concert band has about fifty active members, almost all of whom participate as a side activity. It plays three or four regular concerts during the winter season and weekly during the summer months, usually on the Ithaca Commons (in the atrium of Center Ithaca if it rains) and at the area parks, especially Stewart Park.

Choral music too is a part of the region's musical scene, most of the groups being amateur ensembles. Over the years Cornell University has been a leader in American collegiate choral music, with four active choral groups involving more than two hundred singers, drawn from the student body, the faculty and administration, and the community at large (figure 81). The Cornell Glee

Recreation and Cultural Activities

81. Wilgus Opera House, Ithaca. This performance of G. F. Handel's *Messiah* took place in June 1895 with the combined forces of the Cornell choral groups and the Ithaca Choral Society. Hollis Dann, who since 1889 had been in charge of undergraduate music at Cornell, conducted. Figure 9 shows an exterior view of the opera house.

Club started performing in the late nineteenth century; it is joined in mixed choral work by the Cornell Chorus (of women's voices), started in the 1920s, disbanded, and then revived in 1958, with a regular concert schedule of its own. The Sage Chapel Choir, a mixed chorus providing music for the university's nondenominational Sunday service, has been in existence since the late nineteenth century, and the Cornell Chorale draws on trained musicians from the Cornell and wider community. Ithaca College has both a chorus and a madrigal choir. Most of the principal churches

[183]

around the county have their own choirs. Notable among them is that of Calvary Baptist Church, which for many years has provided black church and gospel music for religious services and many black programs. In addition the Ithaca Community Chorus, open to all interested residents of our region, has been active since the 1970s, and the Ithaca A Cappella, consisting principally of professional and semiprofessional singers, was started in the early 1980s.

Museums and historical societies. The DeWitt Historical Society of Tompkins County (the first local historical society started in 1863, and the present organization was founded in 1935) is located on the first floor of the Clinton House (figures 38 and 87); the museum has changing exhibits, a library and archives, and educational programs. It also puts out historical publications, which are on sale in the museum's shop. It is the county's historical society, with the special functions of collecting manuscripts, archival materials, objects, and photographs and of studying the county's history. Historic Ithaca, founded in 1966 partly as a reaction to the razing of Ithaca's old buildings by urban renewal, is concerned with the already constructed environment—buildings and other man-made structures. It does not collect historical materials. It owns the Clinton House and has its offices there.

The Hinckley Foundation Museum on East Seneca Street houses a collection of nineteenth-century household items. Its changing exhibits focus on the decorative arts and social history of the Finger Lakes region. The Ulysses Historical Society Museum is located in the basement of the Masonic Temple on Main Street, Trumansburg. It is open May through October and has a genealogical research room, which is open by appointment only. The Dryden and Groton historical societies also have museums and mount special exhibits.

The Herbert F. Johnson Museum of Art at Cornell University is the largest museum in the county and houses a permanent collection especially strong in Asian art of the nineteenth and twentieth centuries. The museum also mounts special exhibits and is located in an imposing modern structure, designed by Mario Pei and dominating the northwest corner of the campus. Cornell's art museum

Recreation and Cultural Activities

82. Andrew D. White House on the Cornell Campus.

was for many years housed in the Andrew Dickson White house, a Gothic Revival villa completed in 1873 and designed in part by Ithaca architect William Henry Miller. The house became the residence for successive Cornell presidents until it was put to use as the museum in the 1960s. A south wing was added in 1911, and the building's interior was redecorated in the 1970s; it houses Cornell's Society for the Humanities today (figure 82).

[185]

[6]

Business, Commerce, Industry

INDUSTRIAL and commercial development of any area depends on some universal elements: natural resources, climate and location, and the enterprising spirit of its inhabitants. The story of the commercial development of Tompkins County amply illustrates these factors, but nowhere else in our history, perhaps, do climate and location play such important roles. The weather has dissuaded many businesses from starting up or remaining here; one particularly interesting example is the movie industry, which was lured away from the Ithaca area to sunny southern California, where filming could go on year round. And Tompkins County's terrain—those hills and beautiful gorges—poses a perpetual question. Wonderful sights for tourists are simultaneously colossal problems for developers and commercial interests. Ithaca was seen in the 1830s as a potential commercial center, but geography proved stronger than dreams. Were it not for the rough terrain—and a location removed from both the great industrial centers of the east and major east-west transporation routes—Tompkins County, with Ithaca at its center, might have become a great industrial area. But the railroad through-connection never really worked, and the major markets that many had envisioned never materialized.

Even so, the county has always had its successful small enterprises, and the presence of university and colleges means more business in services and the mercantile trade than in heavy industry. Highly successful commercial ventures have started here,

Business, Commerce, Industry

some unusual and some with real lasting power. Finally, most of the industries started during the very early years to draw upon the natural resources of our region—agriculture, salt, and tourism—are still important today.

Early Development

First settlers throughout the region always looked for two factors: fertile land for their crops and waterpower for their businesses. Early reports speak of Tompkins County's good soil and fine growing conditions (especially in the northern part), and most early settlers farmed the land. Their early crops were wheat, corn, and vegetables, and an early agricultural by-product was potash, manufactured from the residue of the lumber mills (and of the first clearing of the land) and used as fertilizer.

The mills and the boats. Scattered along the major creeks of Tompkins County were mills; waterpower was used to turn mill wheels, and in a few cases the waterways were used to transport logs to the lumber mill. At the beginning there were two basic types of mills, the sawmill and the gristmill. (Flouring mills were few and far between.) In the early days lumbering was a big business, especially in Dryden, and all the communities had mills to grind grain, first for local use and later for sale farther away. Somewhat later mills were built to grind land plaster, or gypsum, which farmers highly regarded as fertilizer. It became one of the county's major products. Brought by barge from the foot of the lake, it was ground in the mills here and then shipped out by wagon.

The early industrial centers of the region developed on Cascadilla, Fall, and Six Mile creeks. Jacob Yaple put up the first mills on Cascadilla Creek near the bottom of the ravine sometime between 1790 and 1800 and used them to grind grain. Up on the hill Otis Eddy built a dam across the creek in 1826 and then a flume to carry water from the dam to Willow Pond; on this site Eddy put up a large cotton factory, which opened in 1827 and employed 60 to 80 people. In 1829 he hired the young Ezra Cornell to work in

[187]

the machine shop. Cotton processing proved unprofitable and was abandoned soon thereafter, but several operating mills and factories remained on the site until they were torn down in 1866. Cascadilla Hall was built near the location of the mills; first a sanatorium, it was taken over by Cornell University (figures 10 and 50). Later, Willow Pond filled in, the dam was allowed to silt over, and the area today is the site of Cornell's Cascadilla tennis courts. At the foot of the creek near Linn Street, meanwhile, a gristmill was built in 1843 which operated until 1902 (fig. 10).

Three different sites were developed on Fall Creek. The area around Ithaca Falls was developed as early as 1813 by Phineas Bennett, first with a gristmill; a plaster mill and a sawmill followed in 1816/7. Soon after came a distillery, which was already doing a booming business in 1822, a tannery, and a small foundry. Water to run the mills was channeled from the creek via a wooden flume, which carried the water from a point above the falls around the face of the bluff and down to the mills. In 1827 Jeremiah Beebe bought 125 acres of land including the gristmill, which he ran until 1830; then he rebuilt it entirely and hired Ezra Cornell, out of a job when the Eddy cotton mill closed, to run the business. Cornell solved the problem of the wooden flume, which, as the area developed, proved inadequate and often broke down. He blasted a tunnel with gunpowder (a remarkable feat, apparently never done before) through which water could be conducted down a raceway to the industry below. The arrangement was subsequently used by the milling and paper companies and, much later, by the Ithaca Gun Company.

The Fall Creek Milling Company was located at the foot of the falls and was in operation from 1830 to 1926 (figure 83). The company turned out the finest grades of flour and distributed them to a wide market. A paper mill was put up in 1819, the first in the county; a successful expanding business, it was extensively damaged by fire in 1846. The company moved to Forest Home for several years and then returned to paper manufacturing at the foot of the falls. In the early 1900s two paper mills were operating in the area. In the early days two kinds of paper were manufactured, and as late as the turn of the century, it is reported, Fall Creek each day ran in different colors, according to the paper being made. Later in

Business, Commerce, Industry

83. Fall Creek Mills (c. 1850).

the twentieth century the Ithaca Paper Company made white paper only; it closed in 1954. The 1840s also saw the establishment of the Ithaca Falls Woolen Manufactory, a large mill with superior machinery which hired thirty-five people, half of whom were women; it manufactured about one hundred yards of fabric per day. Expansion, it was estimated, would treble output, but there was no expansion, and the factory went out of business.

The third site on Fall Creek was at Forest Home (at first called Free Hollow, figure 14), where there was a working mill already in 1794. Joseph Sydney built a gristmill that operated until 1890 (a section of its stone foundation still exists). A woodworking factory was also constructed there, in 1830; it operated until 1926 as the H. J. Bool Furniture Company. In the early days the factory produced fine furniture and provided materials for many of Ithaca's Greek Revival houses. The later Bool Company made furniture, mainly for institutions, and wooden cabinets for the Singer Sewing Machine Company.

Along Six Mile Creek in Ithaca several businesses operated over a period of many years. A gristmill was put up before 1818; it was followed by a carding mill, then a cotton factory. In 1823 a brewery was built on the east side of the creek, below Clinton Street; after changing hands several times it finally burned down in 1878.

The Eagle Factory on the northeast corner of Cayuga and Clinton streets opened in 1824; using waterpower from the creek, its manufactured woolen goods. In 1832 Alvah Beebe erected a stone gristmill on the old Spencer Road, close to the intersection with Cayuga Street, which did considerable business until it burned down. For years the Bostwick family ran a barrel factory on Clinton Street.

Another successful industry was boat building, which started with the organization of the Cayuga Steamboat Company in 1819. The first steamboat on Cayuga Lake, the *Enterprise*, was launched a year later. By 1840 there were between six and ten boat yards in the village of Ithaca, as well as several along the east shore of the lake up to Lansing.

Merchants. Retail merchants rapidly started businesses: by 1834, according to Solomon Southwick's detailed description of Ithaca,[27] Ithaca boasted twenty-three dry goods merchants, three druggists, and sixteen grocers. The earliest merchants often traveled out to bigger commercial centers and brought back goods for the county, usually in exchange for grain. The first merchant in Ithaca was reportedly David Quigg, who arrived about 1800 and traded from a cabin on the south side of Cascadilla Creek. He later moved his goods into a frame building on the southwest corner of Seneca and Aurora streets. In 1853 his two sons moved the business to East State Street, where it continued into the 1890s. Small enterprises of all kinds developed early; as early as 1831 one business was proposing to furnish villagers with bread, delivered daily, more cheaply than they could make it themselves. The merchants—like everyone in those days—lived strenuous lives; the Ithaca Grocery, Provision, Fruit Store & Oyster House, a business that opened in 1823 five doors west of the Ithaca Hotel, advertised sixty-seven items for sale; business operated from December 10 to April 1, from 5 in the morning to 12 at night.

Southwick recorded a great variety of business and industry in 1834. Aside from the retail stores there were thirty-six "mechanical establishments" ranging from tanners and bootmakers to silversmiths, hatters, painters, masons, and carpenters, and a large number of mills and iron foundries, and a chair factory. Soon thereafter, the national panic brought the failure of many businesses and the termination of railroad-building plans—the death of a great commercial dream. It also brought an immediate need for new capital. The businessmen of the community commissioned Ezra Cornell, a local worker with a good reputation, to publicize Ithaca's assets and to bring in new industry. He was unable to do so, however, because Tompkins County was too far from major eastern markets to be appealing as a manufacturing site. It was not until the prosperous 1880s that Ithaca developed further as a commercial center.

The Perennials

Agriculture. Balancing the ups and downs of industry and commerce was the sure and steady element of agriculture. Ithaca's chief trade in the early days was in products related to agriculture products—potash, salt, grain, and cattle. The gristmills and the later flouring companies worked the farms' raw materials, and farmers traded their produce for manufactured goods.

The earliest settlers went to work, first to build themselves shelter and then to clear the land for farming. The trees that were felled went directly into log houses or to the sawmills, which prepared lumber for local building or for export—on lake barges, on wagons, and later on trains—to commercial centers elsewhere in the country. The by-product of all the clearing and sawmilling was potash, which was shipped widely. Early commercial farming was in grain, mostly wheat and corn, the latter being exported mostly in liquid form; by 1835 the county had nine breweries and distilleries turning the grain into liquid spirits, with the by-products being fed to livestock. But farming in the early days was principally self-sufficient; the major problem was to grow enough food for the family, supplemented by abundant fish and wild game. It was not until the Erie Canal was built that produce could be shipped in bulk to consumers in the eastern cities. In the early days beef, mutton, and pork went to market on the hoof. As the local population grew, so did the market for agricultural products, and in 1824 a public market was opened in Ithaca with eight stalls rented at auction. Early products included apple cider and dried apples (apple orchards had been set out as early as 1820), vegetables, and livestock.

The dairy industry developed slowly in Tompkins County, with beef cattle outnumbering dairy cattle for many years. The first marketable dairy products were butter and cheese. Butter was made on the farm and packed in wooden casks weighing about 100 pounds or in 50- to 60-pound tubs. Cheese was a significant manufacture in two communities in the county, McLean and Caroline, where three different butter and cheese factories started up between 1869 and 1873. As cities grew in New York State and transportation simultaneously improved, milk became an important commercial commodity.

One of the most significant changes in farming was the development and application of mechanical power. In those first years the pioneer did the work by hand, clearing the forest with an axe, burning the trees, and planting and harvesting crops among the stumps. Oxen then horses were introduced for the plowing (figure 24). By 1925 the farm census listed 317 tractors in Tompkins County, and in 1964 the census did not even count the workhorse population. Before 1900 horses operated such stationary tools as threshing machines and cider mills; horses also ran the hay press and were used to pull stumps. The real revolution for the farmer and the farm wife took place in the 1930s and 1940s with electric power, which came to operate the milking machine and cool the milk, ventilate the hen house and the dairy barn, run all the other machinery, and, of course, provide light and fuel and power for appliances in the house.

The presence of the State College of Agriculture and Life Sciences at Cornell has had a special impact on the county's farms. Local farmers have been able to consult with specialists in the field and have often been the first to try out new practices. The first calf bred artificially in the state was born on a Trumansburg farm in 1939. Many farm organizations have their headquarters in Ithaca. Agway, which serves twelve states in the northeast with agricultural supplies and tools, was formed in 1964 through a merger of two farm cooperatives, one of which, the Grange League Federa-

Business, Commerce, Industry

tion, had opened its first store in Ithaca in 1924. Other agricultural businesses include the Eastern Artificial Insemination Co-op on East Hill and ISA-Babcock, which breeds and hatches chickens and which has recently leased 145 acres of land near Jacksonville to Natural Lean Pork for the establishment of a pork-raising facility. Also located in Ithaca is the *American Agriculturalist*, a farm paper founded in 1842 and still in circulation.

Farming is still an important industry to Tompkins County. Over the years farmers have adapted to changing times by increasing the size of their farms (thus making fewer farms in the county now than in early days), by mechanizing their operations, by paying more attention to farm management, and by specializing (many farmers, for example, do not raise chickens anymore but buy them from local distributors). And despite national publicity about the decline of the family farm, the one- or two-person farm is still the rule here. Indeed, several local farms are still owned by descendants of pioneer farmers, among them the McLallen farm in the town of Ulysses and the Griswold-Downey farm in Dryden.

And then there is a present-day agricultural success story, the story of the Brown Cow Farm. This yogurt business, which now grosses close to $10 million annually, started in the mid-1970s on a farm in Newfield owned by Tom and Penny Gerhart. They had a Jersey cow that was giving so much extra milk that Penny Gerhart started making yogurt. Soon she was serving it to friends who said she really should sell it; in 1976 she started selling it at the Ithaca Farmers' Market and made about $75 a week. The business grew to twenty-two cows, which the Gerharts eventually sold; there was too much work involved. They then bought the milk, borrowed to put up an extensive plant in 1977, and the Brown Cow Farm on Seely Hill has since grown to twenty-one employees. The yogurt is distributed all over the country, even by air freight to the West Coast, making at most a four-day lapse between production and market. Yet despite all this growth the product has remained unchanged; it is still made with "live" yogurt cultures and with a layer of "yogurt cream" (their trademark) on the top. It is one of those commercial successes, like *The Moosewood Cookbook* or the Morse chain, that has helped put Tompkins County on the map.

Salt. The Indians knew where the salt reservoirs were and they supplied the first settlers. Soon pioneers began to search for salt, and early reports list it as one of the county's leading exports. It was not until the 1880s, however, that the salt industry became a big business. Various borings were made along the lakeshore in the town of Lansing and in 1887 the Cayuga Lake Salt Company was established at Ludlowville. It later became the International Salt Company (figure 84). Around the turn of the century the Remington Salt Company opened a plant near McKinneys, and there was also a salt plant near the end of Third Street in Ithaca; its building was later used as a bag factory for International Salt. In 1916 a salt mine was opened at Myers by John Clute of Watkins Glen, who found a stratum there; the salt was of poor quality, however, and the workings closed. In 1921 the Cayuga Rock Salt Company got the lease of the Clute interest and started mining on the same bed. By drilling just 200 feet deeper they struck it rich; in February 1924 a new bed was found 2,000 feet below the surface of the lake, and it was 99.19 percent pure sodium chloride. Mining extended across the lake and under the hillside along the west shore, and the salt is mined by drilling and blasting. During their peak times the three companies were manufacturing about one thousand tons of salt per day, shipping it out on the Cayuga Lake division of the Lehigh Valley Railroad. Today only the Cayuga Rock Salt Company remains in the area, and it principally mines rock salt for highway departments.

Tourism. The Finger Lakes region is one of the great tourist areas of New York State and of the east, and Tompkins County, with its cluster of state parks and its famous university, is a focal point in the business of tourism.

The hospitality business got an early start in the county. Every small community had its tavern and some a small hotel, especially along the early turnpikes, providing travelers with food and lodging. Davenport's tavern, the Old Stone Heap (figure 85), was a convenient stopping place between Ithaca and Trumansburg. The Old Bush Stand in Caroline was the site of the first town meeting there. Ithaca's first tavern operated in the Abram Markle house on Linn Street (figure 3), the second was opened by Luther Gere in

84. International Salt Company, Lansing. This picture taken at Myers Point shows the company's plant before 1907, when it was destroyed by fire and subsequently rebuilt.

1805 on the southeast corner of Aurora and Seneca streets. Grant's Coffee House, built by a man named Teeter in 1811 as a tavern, was taken over by Jesse Grant and his son. It was destroyed twice by fire and rebuilt each time. When the village and town of Ithaca were incorporated in 1821, Grant's Coffee House served as the village hall, voting place, and trustees' chamber; all municipal officers between 1821 and 1832 were elected there. The Grant & Company stagecoach line also had its office in the building, on the route of the Catskill Turnpike.

The first (and certainly the largest) hotels in the county were the three in Ithaca—the Tompkins House, the Ithaca Hotel, and the elegant Clinton House. They were quickly followed by the Central Exchange Hotel, soon christened Rogues Harbor, and the Dryden Springs House.

A Short History of Tompkins County

85. Old Stone Heap. On the Trumansburg Road, Davenport's tavern is one of the oldest surviving buildings in the county. The third house on the present site (the first two burned), it was put up in 1820.

The Tompkins House was an inn built about 1806 and first called the Ithaca Hotel, on the corner of Aurora and Seneca streets, diagonally across from Gere's tavern; its proprietor, Jacob Vrooman, renamed it Tompkins House in 1809 in honor of New York's popular governor (figure 4). In 1832 a new Tompkins House was built on the same site, a one and one-half story frame building that was later enlarged to four floors (figure 13). Sometime after 1907 it was covered with stucco. The Ithaca Hotel, so named by its builder Luther Gere after Tompkins House got its name, was built in 1809 at the southeast corner of Owego and Aurora streets. This three-story "grand structure" burned in the fire that gutted a large area of the town's center in 1871 and was rebuilt as a four-story brick building in 1872. It had accommodations for 200 guests and 175 diners, and until its demolition in 1967 was a favorite tourist spot, featuring big bands in the 1940s and 1950s (figure 86).

Business, Commerce, Industry

86. Ithaca Hotel. This photograph shows the upstairs hall in 1966, shortly before the building was torn down. See also figure 8.

The most imposing hotel of the area was the Clinton House, which opened in 1830 and was called the grandest hotel west of the Hudson River (figures 38 and 87). Jeremiah S. Beebe, Henry Ackley, and Henry Hibbard built it at an original cost of $22,000. Contemporary reports called it "spacious" and "convenient," words of the highest praise in those days.[28] The building, five stories if one includes basement and attic, was designed in the Greek Revival style and built of brick covered with stucco, with 120 feet of frontage facing east, a grandiose three-story portico, a magnificent staircase, and a cupola that afforded a stunning view of the hillside, lake, and town. The hotel accommodated not only visitors but offices, bathing rooms, spacious halls, and a dining room. Much more than a tourist attraction, the building, with its central location on the park and its meeting rooms, was important for the growth of the village. The building survived several fires and in 1872 was converted to Second Empire style, with a mansard roof; it stayed that way for twenty-five years. It closed as a hotel in 1973

87. Ithaca's Clinton House in 1868. Next to the hotel is the old Clinton Hall, whose third floor auditorium saw many local events, particularly political rallies and vaudeville shows. In figure 38 the Clinton House can be seen in its Second Empire version.

but now, after extensive renovation, lives on as the home of the DeWitt Historical Society, its museum, and archives; it also houses the headquarters of Historic Ithaca, offices, and retail businesses.

Two smaller Ithaca hotels were of particular interest. The Columbian Inn was put up in 1813 on the northwest corner of Owego and Cayuga streets; a murder there in 1831 (a shoemaker named Clark killed his wife and was publicly hanged for the offense) did the business in. The building soon was dismembered; part was moved across the street and became Carson Tavern. The Exchange Hotel, built around 1840 at 124 West State Street, is one of the last remaining frame structures in downtown Ithaca and is probably the second oldest such building remaining in the city.

Business, Commerce, Industry

The Central Exchange Hotel (soon renamed Rogues Harbor, figure 30) was built in the early 1830s at Libertyville (South Lansing) and featured a bar and grillroom on the first floor with sleeping quarters upstairs. It also had a third-floor ballroom with a spring floor. In the 1840s Leap Year Parties were held there, and dances with a country orchestra. The ballroom was the scene of many weddings and celebrations well into the 1900s.

The latter part of the nineteenth century saw the development of many large and elegant hotels throughout Tompkins County: the palatial lakeside hotels that were an essential part of the lake steamer tourist trade, the Taughannock House and the Cataract House hotels at the top of Taughannock Falls, the Phoenix House and the Trembley House in Trumansburg, the Dryden Hotel and the Dryden Springs Place (figure 62), and the watering spas—the Fountain House (figure 16) and the Magnetic Springs House—in Slaterville. Many people of means visited and used these luxurious facilities.

Now, about one hundred years later, the hotels of greatest historical interest in the county are located in old country houses—the Benn Conger Inn in Groton, the Rose Inn (with its spectacular circular staircase) in Lansing, Buttermilk Falls Bed and Breakfast, Glendale Farm (an 1865 farmhouse southwest of Ithaca), all of which offer bed and breakfast accommodations, and the Taughannock Farms Inn.

With four state parks and a great variety of recreational activities, Tompkins County remains a popular center for tourism. Many of its special features have been described in the preceding chapter.

The *Ithaca Journal*. Ithaca's largest daily newspaper is the country's oldest business, and although the city has produced many papers in its history, only the *Journal* remains. The first issue came out in 1815 as an untitled single sheet; according to a report published by the newspaper in 1965 to celebrate its sesquicentennial, evidence points to Ebenezer Mack, a young man of 25 from Owego, as the founder. What is clear is that in 1817 Mack started bringing out a publication named the *American Journal*, and thereafter the paper was printed without interruption, first as a weekly and then, start-

88. Titus Block, Ithaca (c. 1906). The *Ithaca Journal* moved from the Journal Block behind Rothschild's (figure 9) in 1905. The YMCA was housed here for only a short time before it moved to the corner of Buffalo and Tioga streets (figure 93).

ing July 1, 1870, as a daily. Its name was changed to the *Ithaca Journal* in 1824, and over the years it has absorbed many of its competitors. Its first permanent location was on North Tioga Street; it then moved to the Sprague Block on East State Street and to the Culver Block in 1860, and was burned out in both locations. It built its own Journal Block behind the Wilgus Block (which housed the old Rothschild's department store) in 1872 (figure 9). In 1905 it moved to its present location, at that time a Second Empire building known as the Titus Block (figure 88), which it later reconstructed: the top two stories were removed and a brick facade added. In 1912 Frank Gannett, who already owned the *Elmira Star-Gazette*, acquired it, and the *Journal* thus became the second paper of what was to be the Gannett group. A special eight-page feature edition was put out in 1888 to celebrate and commemorate Ithaca's charter as a city, and on May 22, 1965, a special sesquicentennial edition ran to 104 pages. In 1964 came conversion to offset printing, and in 1984 the entire newspaper operation was adapted to computerized makeup and printing. A survey made in 1969 listed 135 different newspapers published to date in Tomkins County.

Corner Book Store. This business has maintained itself in downtown Ithaca ever since its founding in the 1830s. A local history published in 1883 states that D. D. Spencer had established a bookstore more than fifty years earlier, but the location was not specified. Since that time the business has known several different owners and locations, including a building on the corner of State and Tioga streets. When that building was destroyed by fire and replaced by the Finch Block, the bookstore's owner, Dudley Finch, joined in a partnership with a previous owner, George Apgar. The store later was known as Taylor & Carpenter and was incorporated as the Corner Book Store in 1911. It moved to the Blood Building on North Tioga Street in 1923 and to its present site, on South Cayuga Street, in 1969 when the Blood Building was demolished.

Bookstores are an important business in the region and as long as higher education dominates life in Tompkins County, the buying and selling of books will continue to prosper. In and around Ithaca today are twenty bookstores, of which a growing number deal in secondhand and rare books.

Unusual Enterprises

Groton. Industrial areas developed in and close to Ithaca in the nineteenth century, and mills and a few woolen factories were scattered through the county. The only other important industries sprang up in Groton. The most notable of these were an iron foundry that developed into a bridge company, a carriage business, and an innovative typewriter company. All three were started in the late nineteenth century with enormous success; two have since been taken over by larger companies.

The Groton Carriage Company was incorporated as a carriage works in 1876. It was the outgrowth of a business established about 1855, and during its years of manufacturing, up to 1910, the company made many different vehicles, some exceedingly elegant. Their cutters, carriages, carts, and delivery wagons were sold all over the country (see figure 26). With the growth in popularity of the automobile, the company went out of business.

The Groton Bridge & Manufacturing Company between the years 1877 and 1921 was the most important iron foundry in the county, although there were smaller foundries in Ithaca earlier in the nineteenth century. An outgrowth of the Groton Iron Works, which started in 1849 and made agricultural implements and machinery, this firm began making iron bridges in 1877. Ten years later it combined several small iron-work industries into one of the largest firms building iron bridges in the United States (figure 40). It later merged with the American Bridge Company.

The best-known endeavor of the three was the manufacture of typewriters, which began late in the nineteenth century. The Crandall Machine Company operated between 1881 and 1905 and developed a typewriter that won a gold medal at the Paris Exposition in 1893. Business declined with the development of more efficient machines, but the idea of making typewriters persisted in the region. In 1909 the Rose Typewriter Company of New York City moved to Groton and took over buildings vacated by the carriage company. Rose manufactured a typewriter called the Standard Folding Machine (figure 89), which had interchangeable type and therefore great potential for foreign markets. The name was changed in 1912 to Corona—the "crown" of typewriters on the international market. The machine was also compact and light (it weighed only six pounds) and was known for its durability; it was widely bought and used during World War I. In 1925 the company merged with the L. C. Smith Typewriter Company of Syracuse, and a final merger was made with W. Marchant Calculators in 1958, forming the giant corporation Smith Corona Marchant,

Business, Commerce, Industry

89. Standard Folding Typewriter. This is just one example of Groton's unusual enterprises. For others, see figures 26 and 40.

which today is moving into the manufacture of data-processing equipment. SCM has recently shut down its Groton typewriter assembly plant. The buildings have been demolished, and future plans for the site are not settled.

Ithaca. Several small and highly diversified businesses operated with great success in Ithaca during the second half of the nineteenth century. Many eventually had to close, however; in 1890, 80 firms sold $1,786,000 in products, but by 1919 the number had dropped to 72 while the value had increased enormously, to $9,935,000. The Ithaca Manufacturing Works operated for about twenty years at the present location of the Ithaca Gun Company, making agricultural implements mostly. Reynolds & Lang, which started in 1868, produced agricultural implements and traction engines first on Tioga and then on Green Street until it closed in 1954. Ithaca had several cigar manufactories (Newfield also had one); among them was A. H. Platts & Company, which began in 1863 and occupied all four floors of one part of the Grant Block on East State Street. It employed as many as forty cigar makers at one time and produced several famous brands, but the introduction of ready-made cigarettes in the 1890s drove cigar companies out of business. A glass factory, one of Ezra Cornell's last financial ventures, was established on Third Street in 1874; it ceased operations in 1892. The Ithaca Organ Company—which made reed organs for church and parlor use—started up in 1877 and went bankrupt in 1885. The Autophone Company in 1879 started manufacturing automatic organs, patented by Henry B. Horton, inventor of the improved calendar clock; by 1900 the company was making roller organs, which were also automatic instruments, as well as music rolls and sheets for them. It closed in 1925. The Ithaca Sign Works Company, which started up in the early 1900s, grew rapidly and became Ithaca's largest industry by 1926. The Ithaca Sign Works Building, standing next to the flood control channel, has housed various businesses since the sign company closed, but at present stands vacant.

One of Ithaca's best-known industries, the Ithaca Calendar Clock Company, appears to have begun operations in 1866 with the invention of the new perpetual calendar, invented by Henry B. Horton. The first calendar clock, an invention of J. H. Hawes in 1853, had one problem: it had no February 29th. This defect was corrected in 1854 by W. H. Akins, who lived in Speedsville. The company started out in one room at 101 West State Street (now the Chanticleer Bar) and, after several moves in downtown Ithaca, located in 1874 in a new, three-story brick building on the site of the old county fairgrounds at Dey and Adams streets. The building burned in 1876 and was promptly rebuilt (figure 90). It is still in use today, housing the Clever Hans Bakery, The Circuit Tree, and a bookstore; for several years now, its second floor has hosted the annual Friends of the Library book sale. The Ithaca calendar clock enjoyed worldwide popularity, and the company manufactured forty-five different styles. The firm went bankrupt soon after Pro-

Business, Commerce, Industry

90. Ithaca Calendar Clock Factory (c. 1900).

hibition began—principally because among its largest markets were breweries and distilleries, which gave clocks away as premiums—and closed around 1921. The story has a sequel, however, for the Ithaca Calendar Clock Company started up again in 1981, with headquarters on Taughannock Boulevard; they make up to two hundred clocks per year in six different models, ranging in price from $900 to $4,000.

Another famous industry of the area was movie making, and for about five years Ithaca was a center of unusual excitement and a certain enchantment. Lavishly dressed movie personalities strolled around in downtown Ithaca and drove flashy cars, creating a glamorous local spectacle. Many area residents got to play as extras in crowd scenes. Theodore and Leopold Wharton came with their film company, Wharton Studios, in about 1914. The company specialized in short films, especially continuing serials—comedy, suspense, and horror stories mostly—and did considerable

91. *The Great White Trail*. This scene is from one of the many movies shot in the county by the Wharton Studios and which made good use of the local terrain for a dramatic setting.

amounts of news and propaganda filming, especially in 1917 and 1918. They set up their "location" on the edge of the lake in Renwick Park and made use of many local scenes in their films (figure 91). Probably the most famous movie filmed in Ithaca was *The Exploits of Elaine*, which starred Pearl White. The company also made a famous shot of an old street car running off the Stewart Avenue Bridge and making a 200-foot plunge into Fall Creek Gorge, and at one time tried to purchase the former Dryden Springs Place, which was an elegantly furnished building, to make a movie there. The graceful and gifted dancer and actress Irene Castle starred in *Patria*, a patriotic serial in fifteen episodes, which she filmed following the death of her husband and dancing partner, Vernon Castle. In 1919 Irene Castle came to live in Ithaca as the wife of Robert E. Treman (son of Robert H. and brother of Allan H.). They lived in a large greystone house in the Heights (today the Sigma Chi fraternity house), which had the first private swimming pool in town. Several years later Irene Castle, who had given over most of her financial resources to independent movie making, left to resume her career on the stage, thus terminating both her marriage and her relationship to Ithaca.

Large and Small Successes

Morse Chain, NCR, Ithaca Gun. A lasting big business in Tompkins County has been the Morse Chain Company, now part of a multimillion dollar international enterprise, Morse Borg-Warner. It started out as the Morse Spring Company, part of the Gregg Iron Works in Trumansburg, in the early 1890s. Everett Fleet Morse and his brother Frank worked together to produce a new style of cart spring for two-wheeled carts. In 1893 Fleet Morse set out to perfect a durable bicycle chain (he was once quoted as saying, "I believe I can make a better chain than that"), one with a rocker joint to reduce friction, and by the mid-1890s the bicycle chain had replaced cart springs as the company's major product.[29] Toward the end of the century Frank Morse adapted the design for high-speed power transmission, and in 1898 the Morse brothers incorporated their business. Frank Morse then developed a toothed silent chain used in the early automobile. The business expanded rapidly, outgrew the old Gregg Iron Works Building, and moved in 1905 to a new factory built on Ithaca's South Hill. The plant grew to become part of the Borg-Warner Corporation in 1928. In the early 1980s Morse Borg-Warner moved to a large modern facility on Warren Road in Lansing, which contains an administrative building, an advanced engineering lab, and a plant that makes engine and transmission chains. The company has business locations all over the world.

What stands out in the history of this enterprise is not only the industry and inventiveness of its owners but also their ability to adapt and to diversify their business. They built aircraft, under the name Thomas-Morse Aircraft Corporation (which leased the old airport area now part of Cass Park); it was later sold to Bell Aircraft Company. The Barr-Morse Company, added to the enterprise in 1923, made a portable typewriter with standard keyboard. Frank Morse also involved the company in the Poole clock (which ran on three flashlight batteries), a pocket calculator, and a bridge table with a built-in scoring device. None of these products had any great success.

One sideline of Frank Morse did endure: it was the adding machine. In 1919 a man named Hefer Cushing Peters completed an adding machine model; he met up with Frank Morse who at the time was looking for new items to diversify his product line. An agreement was reached between the two: Morse was to perfect, tool, build, and market the machine, which would carry the Peters name. The Peters-Morse Manufacturing Company had machines ready for the market in 1921, but it lacked a full sales organization. In the late 1920s Morse joined forces with another company with no assets but a good sales force; Morse would build the machines and the new organization, the Allen-Wales Corporation, would sell them. After the financial crises of 1929 the adding machine division of Morse Industries and Allen-Wales officially merged, and the combined operation, the Allen-Wales Adding Machine Corporation, became extremely successful. With the advent of World War II, 85 percent of the factory turned to manufacture war items; the company was purchased by the National Cash Register Company in 1943 and became its adding machine division.

NCR has been located on South Hill in Ithaca since 1943. After acquiring Allen-Wales, it manufactured adding machines and a new factory was built in 1957/8 for the adding machine division. Today NCR provides printers for many NCR projects and has become a large manufacturer of computers. It has introduced a new medical computer, designed and manufactured in Ithaca. It also makes microcomputer stations, information systems for hospitals, restaurants, stores, and banks, and "customer-activated retail devices" (machines that use cards) for airlines, hotels, convenience stores, gas stations, and, of course, banks.

The Ithaca Gun Company was started by LeRoy Smith, brother of the L. C. Smith who ran the typewriter company, and W.

Henry Baker of Brooktondale, an inventor and gunsmith. The two men came to Ithaca in 1880 because of its waterpower and set up shop in an old factory near the Ithaca Falls which had manufactured agricultural machinery. In the early years the company made about 3,000 guns per year; the business prospered and by the 1920s was making about 52,000 guns annually, more than one-half of the double-barreled hammerless guns sold in the United States. It gained worldwide recognition for its finely handcrafted products. In recent years the Ithaca Gun Company has encountered considerable financial difficulties, and its future is unclear.

Professions. The various professions have prospered in the county. The medical and dental professions have already been discussed. The legal profession has had a rather quiet life during the county's history. The first lawyers—and there were quite a few—dealt chiefly with conflicting and dubious land titles. When the county was formed in 1817, the first bench was appointed; in addition, the county's offices all had a legal or law-enforcement flavor—the first officials were First Judge, Surrogate, Clerk, Sheriff, and District Attorney. In the village of Ithaca's first twenty years, more than half its presidents were members of the legal profession. In 1818 the county built its first courthouse (figure 5) on Mill Street, on land given to the county by Simeon DeWitt. A rapidly constructed wooden building in Greek Revival style, it was replaced by the old Tompkins County Courthouse, begun in 1854 and occupied in 1855; the building cost $12,154.76. After the present courthouse (just two buildings to the east) was constructed in 1932, the old courthouse housed county offices. The oldest public building in Tompkins County and the oldest Gothic Revival courthouse in the state, it was completely renovated in 1975/6 as a Bicentennial project (figure 92). The second-floor courtroom originally had a cathedral ceiling, which was blocked off in Victorian times to reduce heating costs.

The present Neo-Georgian courthouse is located to the east of the corner of Court and Tioga streets and has on record all the county's wills, deeds, and legal documents. Lawyers who practice in the county must be admitted to the New York State Bar, or if members of another state bar must pass examination by the Board

A Short History of Tompkins County

92. Old Tompkins County Courthouse, Ithaca (c. 1870). The building to the right was the county jail until the 1930s. This photograph and figure 68 were taken by Joseph C. Burritt.

of Law Examiners for New York State. The county is under the jurisdiction of one of the state's regional Appellate Divisions. The Tompkins County Bar Association has about seventy members today, who hold a monthly luncheon meeting. The county's lawyers compete against the county's doctors in an annual basketball game between "Jawbones" and "Sawbones" which raises money for community agencies.

The banking business got an early start in Ithaca and has known considerable prosperity. The first bank on the scene was the Bank of Newburgh, which established a branch in Ithaca before 1820 and a few years later built a handsome office on West State Street on a lot given for the purpose by Simeon DeWitt. The building, probably the oldest still standing in Ithaca, was moved to East Court Street in 1912 to be used as the parsonage of the First Baptist

Business, Commerce, Industry

Church. The Bank of Ithaca (or the Ithaca Bank) was chartered in 1829 and opened offices in the Colonial Building, completed after 1830 and the oldest building on the Commons; it took over the branch office of the Bank of Newburgh in 1830 and in 1849 merged with the Tompkins County Bank. The present Tompkins County Trust Company started out in 1836 as the Tompkins County Bank. It merged in 1935 with the Ithaca Trust Company (founded in 1891) and at that time adopted its present name. It operates branch banks today in Dryden, Trumansburg, Lansing (at the Triphammer Mall), and at several locations in Ithaca. The First National Bank of Ithaca organized in 1864, opened its first office on East State Street and then moved to the Cornell Public Library (figure 60). It merged nine years later with the Merchants & Farmers Bank, organized in 1838. In 1981 the bank was purchased by Security New York State Corporation of Rochester, which subsequently merged with a larger holding company from Albany, Norstar Bancorp, and changed its name first to Security Trust Company, then to Security Norstar. The present Citizens Saving Bank was founded in 1868 as the Ithaca Savings Bank and had its first offices in a drugstore on State Street. It occupies today the site of Woodcock House, the home of Alonzo Cornell, governor of New York State and son of Ezra Cornell, the bank's first president (figure 60). More recent banking institutions in the county include Ithaca Savings & Loan, an affiliate of the First Federal Savings & Loan Association of Rochester, and several credit unions.

Among recent commercial successes are a growing number of computer and other high-technology industries devoted to research and development, especially in aerospace and science, and to the marketing of high-tech products. Cornell University and the Tompkins County Area Development Corporation (a private, not-for-profit organization dedicated to creating and conserving jobs in the county by investing in and helping local businesses) created a Research Park next to the Tompkins County Airport a few years ago and have developed a research complex there. The facilities have been leased at an attractive price by the university, which provides support services, access to its facilities, and other resources. This environment has helped very sophisticated high-tech companies proliferate in the region. Elsewhere at least a dozen new businesses start up in the county every year, and quite frequently established businesses change hands and keep on going.

The center of the major retail scene in Tompkins County is the village of Lansing with its four malls, the largest being Pyramid Mall, which houses more than seventy businesses under one roof. The Ithaca Commons has a new large store built by Rothschild's, a department store that operated for one hundred years before closing in 1982, and now operated by the S. F. Iszard Company; a recent and newly reconstructed Center Ithaca; many new and old businesses behind refurbished storefronts; play areas, site furniture, and attractive planting. The city's other shopping centers include the DeWitt Mall (adapted from the old high school) and the newly renovated Clinton West, also an adaptation (of the former Co-op Food Store & Shopping Center).

The Tompkins County Chamber of Commerce was founded in 1888 as the Board of Trade; in 1925 the Ithaca Business Men's Association became a part of the organization. Housed in an elegant building on Court Street dating from before 1873, the chamber has available brochures and publications about the region, and during the summer months operates a tourist information booth at the entrance to Stewart Park. Thus the chamber promotes two of the county's important and perennial industries—tourism and mercantile trade.

Afterword: Past to Present

AFTER looking at Tompkins County from its origins to the present day, over a period of almost two hundred years, one wants to look into the future, to see what it holds for us and our surroundings. We cannot do that, of course, and especially in these uncertain times it makes little sense even to attempt a look ahead. Nevertheless, some recent developments in our story will have reasonably predictable results. We can see greater growth coming in high technology, for example, especially with Cornell University's increasing prominence in the field and with state funding for biotechnology. Our institutions of higher learning will continue to expand. We can see more commercial development, more houses, more people.

A glance at population figures for Tompkins County is rather startling. One assumes that the population grew during the nineteenth century, when in reality it dropped between 1835 and 1845 and again between 1850 and 1865 (although part of that drop can be attributed to jurisdictional changes and the Civil War). The population in 1890 was 32,923, a figure very close to that of 1835, which was 32,345. The nineteenth-century figures show so little change that when we speak of growth, we really mean development. The scene in 1835 was vastly different from that of 1890, and one has only to visualize the central commercial area of Ithaca at those two moments to understand the meaning of change. And, of course, all those enormous changes in appearance match more important changes—in living conditions, occupations, ways of life.

A Short History of Tompkins County

The county really didn't grow until after World War II, with a jump from 42,340 in 1940 to 59,122 in 1950 (it was over 77,000 in 1970). The more recent numbers, however, also reflect the inclusion of students in the census as of the 1940s.

Looking back on the past of Tompkins County should really make us much more aware of the present—perhaps to look at things differently, perhaps simply to see more than we used to. If the past teaches us anything, it teaches us that our historical heritage is of prime importance and that we should be more mindful of its preservation. The development of historical museums and societies, the great interest in genealogy and in tracing the past, the concept of historic preservation of buildings and traditions all serve to make us more aware of the importance of our past. In 1942 the John D. Rockefeller Foundation established a Collection of Regional History at Cornell University, with quarters in Olin Library's Department of Manuscripts and University Archives. Historic Ithaca was founded in 1966 with offices in the beautifully restored and renewed Clinton House. This building, very important in Tompkins County's past, today continues to play a central role in keeping this past alive and is both the symbol and embodiment of our architectural and historical tradition. The preservation of old buildings has not always been of great concern, as much of Ithaca's urban renewal around 1960 testifies (figure 93). More recently, the community has gone through the seemingly endless drama of the Boardman House, with every month a new act being written and new scenes to play out. The drama did eventually come to an end, however, and a happy end at that, with renovation and a new role as an office building.

Keeping in mind the importance of solving the questions of preserving our heritage, we must look ahead to the solution of certain perennial problems for the county—what to do with the Farmers' Market (which provides an outlet for produce from all sides of the county), what to do about Route 96, what to do with the Strand Theatre. And we must consider more serious problems as well—what to do about the county's social ills, how to find solutions for its badly neglected and impoverished areas, for example.

When I set out to research this history of Tompkins County, I wanted very much to find elements in the past which would tell

Afterword: Past to Present

93. Old City Hall, Ithaca (1923). This photograph also shows the post office, with the YMCA behind. To the left of the cupola is the spire of the Unitarian Church and in the right foreground is the Cornell Public Library. Of these buildings only the post office and the church are still standing today.

me what makes our rich environment unique. I did find certain durable threads in the tapestry: the beautiful terrain, the climate (both outdoor and intellectual), and—above all—the people, people who have through the years shown extraordinary ability for adaptation, ingenuity, and determination. Our county is what it is today first and foremost because of the dedication and creativity of its residents, past and present.

Notes

1. Quoted in W. Glenn Norris, *Early Explorers and Travelers* (Ithaca, 1961), pp. 45, 46.
2. See Henry Edward Abt, *Ithaca* (Ithaca, 1926), pp. 26–27.
3. Letter of 18 February 1810, in William Heidt, *Simeon DeWitt* (Ithaca, 1968), p. 47; further details are given on p. 48.
4. Quoted by Evelyn Schuyler Schaeffer, *From Sunrise to Sunset* (Cornell University, Department of Manuscripts and University Archives).
5. The mansion was completed in the autumn of 1881, at a reputed cost of nearly $300,000, and was lavishly furnished and decorated with fine art and furniture that the Fiskes had sent back from their travels in Europe and Asia. Jennie McGraw Fiske never lived in this splendid residence (when she returned to Ithaca in 1881 she was near death). It was taken over by Chi Psi fraternity and in 1906 was destroyed by fire, leaving only a memory of almost unbelievable opulence.
   Many of Ithaca's residential and commercial buildings downtown and on East Hill are discussed and depicted in Daniel R. Snodderly, *Ithaca and Its Past* (Ithaca, rev. ed., 1984); Kermit Carlyle Parsons, *The Cornell Campus* (Ithaca, 1968); and Merrill Hesch and Richard Pieper, *Ithaca Then and Now* (Ithaca, 1983).
6. See Carol Kammen, ed., *What They Wrote: 19th Century Documents from Tompkins County, New York* (Ithaca, 1978), p. 25. Henceforth cited as *What They Wrote*.
7. The quote is from a historical sketch made in 1876 by J. M. Farrington and based on Hermon Camp's accounts. See John H. Selkreg, *Landmarks of Tompkins County* (Syracuse, 1894), p. 211.
8. *Ithaca Chronicle* from April 10, 1834, and cited by Hardy Campbell Lee, *A History of Railroads in Tompkins County* (Ithaca, 1977), p. 10.

9. Ibid., p. 11.

10. *Autobiography of Andrew D. White* (New York, 1905), I, 294. White described Cornell as "austere and reserved in appearance," as a person with a "warm heart and noble purpose" (p. 298).

11. The words of the eloquent orator who described the great works of Ezra Cornell were repeated by Goldwin Smith to A. D. White: ". . . he came up to this height [and here came a great wave of the hand over the vast amphitheater below and around us] and he established this *universe!*" (*Autobiography*, I, 386).

12. Quoted by Morris Bishop, *A History of Cornell* (Ithaca, 1962), p. 91.

13. See *Autobiography*, I, 340.

14. From a letter written by the father of D. Willard Fiske, Cornell professor and university librarian, in *What They Wrote*, p. 121.

15. *What They Wrote*, p. 122.

16. From the diary of James Rawlins, dated Ithaca Falls, October 19, 1873, in *What They Wrote*, p. 117.

17. See Paul Bradford's account in Carol Kammen, *Lives Passed: Biographical Sketches from Central New York* (Interlaken, N.Y., 1984), p. 147.

18. *Dedication of the Cornell Library Building*, pp. 1, 5–12, 16.

19. See the accounts of the Reverend Samuel Parker in *What They Wrote*, pp. 13 and 18. Solomon Southwick (who described himself as an "impartial observer") in 1834 painted a rather different picture: "There are about 50 large religious societies; and every family is supplied with a Bible" (p. 43).

20. See *What They Wrote*, p. 57.

21. DeWitt Clinton's diary from August 10, 1810, in *What They Wrote*, p. 15; other accounts from 1829 and 1830 are on pages 37 and 47. Also Solomon Southwick's description of the region fairly gushes with enthusiasm.

22. From a memoir of Reverend Parker in *What They Wrote*, p. 13.

23. *Autobiography*, I, 352.

24. Quoted in Heidt, *Simeon DeWitt*, p. 38; another similar description can be found in *What They Wrote*, p. 47.

25. D. H. Fiske's letter in *What They Wrote*, p. 122.

26. From Kammen, *Lives Passed*, p. 144.

27. Quoted in *History of Tompkins County New York*, p. 76.

28. From an 1830s article in *The Casket*, a literary magazine; quoted in *What They Wrote*, p. 57.

29. From an account by one of the Morse brothers in *What They Wrote*, p. 133.

Bibliography

Abt, Henry Edward. *Ithaca*. Ithaca: Ross W. Kellogg, 1926.
Bishop, Morris. *A History of Cornell*. Ithaca: Cornell University Press, 1962.
Burns, Thomas W. *Initial Ithacans*. Ithaca: Press of the Ithaca Journal, 1904.
Child, Hamilton, ed. *Gazetteer and Business Directory of Tompkins County, N.Y. for 1868*. Syracuse: Journal Office, 1868.
Cloyes, Samuel A. *The Healer*. The Story of Dr. Samantha S. Nivison and Dryden Springs, 1820–1915. Ithaca: DeWitt Historical Society, 1969.
———. *Beyond the Footlights*. Story of the Dryden Opera House, 1893–1936. Ithaca: DeWitt Historical Society, 1968.
Dedication of the Cornell Library Building. Ithaca, N.Y. December 20, 1866. New York: American Photo-Lithographic Co., 1867.
Ellis, David W., et al. *A History of New York State*. Ithaca: Cornell University Press, rev. ed., 1967.
Gallway, Sydney H. *Underground Railroad in Tompkins County*. Ithaca: DeWitt Historical Society, 1963.
Heidt, William, Jr., ed. *Carrie Manning's Diary, 1869*. Ithaca: DeWitt Historical Society, 1962.
———. *Simeon DeWitt, Founder of Ithaca*. Ed. Carol Kammen. Ithaca: DeWitt Historical Society, 1968.
Hesch, Merrill, and Richard Pieper. *Ithaca Then and Now*. Ithaca: McBooks, 1983.
History of Tompkins County New York. Philadelphia: Everts & Ensign, 1879. Repr. Ovid, N.Y. W. E. Morrison, 1976.

The Ithaca Journal. "The Journal's 150 Years." Anniversary Edition. May 22, 1965.

Kammen, Carol. *Lives Passed: Biographical Sketches from Central New York.* Interlaken, N.Y.: Heart of the Lakes, 1984.

——, ed. *What They Wrote: 19th Century Documents from Tompkins County, New York.* Ithaca: Cornell University, Department of Manuscripts and University Archives, 1978.

Lee, Hardy Campbell. *A History of Railroads in Tompkins County.* Rev. and enlarged by Winton Rossiter. Ithaca: DeWitt Historical Society, 1977.

Newfield—150 Years (1822–1972). Ithaca: Art Craft of Ithaca, 1973.

Noble, Helen B. *Reminiscing through Four Generations.* Ithaca: Art Craft of Ithaca, 1945.

Norris, W. Glenn. *Early Explorers and Travelers in Tompkins County.* Ithaca: DeWitt Historical Society, 1961.

Parish, Isabelle H. *This, Too, Happened in Lansing.* Ithaca: DeWitt Historical Society, 1967.

Parsons, Kermit Carlyle. *The Cornell Campus.* Ithaca: Cornell University Press, 1968.

Pritchard, Zelle Middaugh. *Ellis Hollow Lore.* Ithaca: DeWitt Historical Society, 1962.

Sears, Lydia. *A History of Trumansburg, New York, 1792–1967.* Ithaca: Art Craft of Ithaca, 1968.

Selkreg, John H. *Landmarks of Tompkins County.* Syracuse: D. Mason, 1894.

Snodderly, Daniel R. *Ithaca and Its Past.* Rev. ed. Ithaca: DeWitt Historical Society, 1984.

Southwick, Solomon. *Views of Ithaca and Its Environs by an Impartial Observer.* Ithaca: n.p., 1835.

The Spirit of Enterprise: Nineteenth Century in Tompkins County. Compiled by Gretchen Sachse, Janet Mara, and Gretel Leed. Ithaca: DeWitt Historical Society & Hinckley Foundation Museum, 1977.

White, Andrew D. *Autobiography of Andrew D. White.* 2 vols. New York: Century, 1905.

Index

Page references to illustrations appear in italic type.

agricultural societies, 65, 112, 171–72
agriculture, 63, 69; changes in, 192–93; dairy industry, 59, 70, 81, 192, 193; early, 34–36, 187, 192; education, 112, 114–15, 118, 192; family farming, 65, 82, 193; organizations in, 192–93; products, 35, 74, 187, 191–92; shipping and trade in, 37, 42, 77, 95, 187, 191–92. *See also* fairs
airport: hangar, 163, 164, 179; municipal, 17, 161, 163, 208; Tompkins County, 73, 87, 104, 107, *109*, 211
alcoholism, 56, 74, 76, 77, 82, 84, 137–38
Allen-Wales Adding Machine Corporation, 208
American Agriculturalist, 15, 193
Anthony, William, 44, 108–9, 110
Applegate Corners, 68–69
Atwaters, excursions to, 100, 169
auditoriums, 135, 177, *178*, 180, *183*, *198*

Bagnardi, J. Victor, 134
Bahar, Hushang, 125
Bailey, Liberty Hyde, 118
Baker, Judah, 68
Baker, Samuel, 74, 95
bands, 70, 77, 180–82, *182*; concerts by, 100, 161, 170; pavilions and

bandstands, 158–59, *159*, *162*, 180, 181
banks, 82, *136*, 210–11; Bank of Newburgh, 31, 210–11; Tompkins County Trust Company, 145, 178, 211
Bates, Daniel, 12, 41
Bath & Jericho Turnpike. *See* Catskill Turnpike
Beebe, Elizabeth, 147, *148*
Beebe, Jeremiah S., 112, 188, 197
Beebe Lake, 93, 112, 173, *174*
Beers, Dr. Lewis, 60–61, 140, 145, 150, 155
Bergholtz, Herman, 12, 51, 105, 160, 161
Besemer, depot at, 58, 59
Besemer, Josiah, 59
black(s), 16; history and culture, 152, 184. *See also* slaves
Bloodgood, Abraham, land of, 29, 31
Bloodgood, Francis, 29, 154
Boardman House, 16, 43, 44, 53, 120, 122, 214
Bostwick House, 144, *145*
bridges, 52–53; across gorges, 52, 54, 92, 92–93, 105; covered, 15, 59, *60*, 79–80, 84, *85*, 93, *94*; early, 72, 89, 91; railroad, 57, *57*, 100, *101*; trolley, 93, 105. *See also* industries; Stewart Avenue; Triphammer Bridge

[221]

Index

Brooktondale, 56–57, 107; railroad bridge, 57, 57, 100, *101*
Brown Cow Farm, 81, 193
Brown, Solyman, 145
Brule, Etienne, 14, 24
Bush, Richard, 57–58
Butler, William, 25
Buttermilk: Creek, 22, 24–25, 61, 97; Falls State Park, 18, 165, *166*

Cammerhof, John Frederick, 24
Camp, Hermon, 82, 89; mansion of, 15, 82, *83*
Cantine, John (General), 56, 58, 60
Caroline, town of: annexed to county, 15, 37; industries, 56, 192; organization, 14, 59; role in transportation, 34, 54, 58; settlement of, 33, 55, 57–59; small communities in, 58
Cascadilla Creek, 22, 98, 190; boat landings, *48–49*, 94, 95, *170*; bridges over, 92–93; dam across, 187–88; mills, 27, 31, 41, 47, 112, 116, 187–88
Cascadilla Hall, 16, 47, 112, *117*, 126, 188; and early Cornell, 116, 141–42; as sanatorium, 141–42
Cass Park, 19, 160, 163; land for, 162–63, 208
Castle, Irene, 206–7
Catskill Turnpike, 54; charter for, 14, 34; route of, 34, 45, 69, *90*, 91, 95, 104, 195
Cayuga Bridge, 42, 95, 154, 169
Cayuga Chamber Orchestra, 180
Cayuga Heights, 17, 31, 38, 55, 105–6, 151, 160
Cayuga Indians. *See* Indians
Cayuga Lake, 16, 17, 24; excursions on, 42, 95, 100, 161, 168–70; formation, 21–22; link to Erie Canal, 15, 42, 93–94, 96, 104; parks at head of, 160, 162, 170
Cayuga Steamboat Company, 95, 190
Cayuta, 33; annexed to county, 15, 36, 80
Central Exchange Hotel. *See* Rogues Harbor Inn
church(es): Beebe Mission House, 147, *148*; Congregational (West Groton), 73, 73; Danby Federated, 61, *150*, 150; Ithaca, 39, *88*, *122*, 151–52, 158, *215*; St. James AME, 15, 152, *153*, 154. *See also* Presbyterian Church
church organizations: early, 61, 65, 69, 71, 74, 83; Baptists, 83, 150, 152; Congregationalists, 73, 151; Methodists, 150, 151; Quakers, 152, 154; Reformed Dutch, 58, 150, 151; Swedenborgian, 61, 145, 150
Civil War, 16, 42, 83, 146, 213; monument in Danby, 61, *63*, 63
Clark, Daniel, 74
Clinton House, 15, 31, 42, *88*, 91, 117, 195, *198*; building of, 97; description, 47, 197; importance, 214; renovation and adaptation, 53, 184, 198
Cobb, Amasa, 72
Cobb, Lyman, *Cobb's Spelling-Book*, 58
commercial buildings, 43, 45–46, 47, 201; Finch Block, *136*, 201; Journal Block, 43, *46*, 200; Opera Block (Trumansburg), *86*, 86; Titus Block, 128, 174, *200*, 200–201; Wilgus Block, 16, 43, *46*, 120, *136*, *168*, 177, *183*
community centers, 67, 175
community service organizations: benevolent, 146–47; women's, 147–49
Connecticut Hill, 78, 81
Conway, Patrick, 161, 181–82, *182*
Coon, Levi, 54
Coreorgonel, 24–25
Cornell, Ezra, 12, 16, *113*, 211, 218n10; arrival in Ithaca, 15, 42, 112; business ventures of, 42, 98, 100, 112, 204; occupations, 42, 108, 112, 115, 188, 191; plans for Cornell University, 115, 117, 218n11. *See also* Cornell Public Library
Cornell Heights, 93, 105, 160, 207
Cornell Public Library, 19, 42, 134, *136*, *215*; dedication, 16, 135; incorporation, 112, 114, 135; special functions, 107, 135, 174, 177, 211
Cornell University, 39, 102, 214; as coeducational, 18, 117–18; develop-

[222]

ment, 43, 118–20; early days, 116–117; faculty, 18, 19, 118, 175; founding, 16, 42, 114–15; importance, 112, 120; recreational areas and activities, 102, *103*, *173*, 173, *174*, 179–80; schools and colleges at, 18, 19, 118–20, *119*, 140, 192

Cornell University campus: Andrew D. White House, 47, *185*, 185; buildings, 44, *47*, 47, *48–49*, *50*, *116*, 116, 120, *157*; chimes mechanism, 65, 115, *116*, 120; Herbert F. Johnson Museum, 185; street railway on, 105

Corner Book Store, *136*, 201

creeks: principal, in county, 22; and waterpower, 22, 27, 31, 33, 41, 54, 56, 59, 69, 74, 93, 187. *See also names of creeks*

Danby, town of: *62*, 64, 150; annexed to county, 15, 37, 61; organization, 14, 61; schools in, 61, 128, 131; settlement of, 28, 33, 60–61; small communities in, 61; Town Hall and monument, 61, *63*, 63

Dann, Hollis, *176*, *183*

Davenport's tavern (Old Stone Heap), 82, 194, *196*

Dean, Eliaken, 33, 78–79

Dearborn, Henry, 24, 82

DeWitt Building: modern adaptation, 47, 52, 53, 130–31, 212; as school site, 125, 129, 130

DeWitt Park, *44*, 134; bandstand in, *159*, 180; as college campus, 120–21, *122*, 158; early settlement, 14, 27; as public square, 41, 157–58

DeWitt, Simeon, *28*, 112, 151; contributions to county, 31, *36*, 209, 210; death, 15, 31, 158; and establishment of Ithaca, 12, 28–31, 151, 157–58; maps by, 14, 29, *30*, 31, views on agricultual education, 114–15

Division, town of, 15, 38, 70

Dryden Springs House, 141, *195*, *199*; as sanatorium, 16, 64, 141–42, *142*, 206

Dryden, town of: 15, 25, 34, 38, *133*, *142*, 180; boundaries, 63–64; communities in, 64; formation, 14, 64, 65; incorporated village named, 16, 38, 64; industries, 64, 187; parks, 158–59; settlement of, 33, 64, 133; schools in, 15, 33, 64, *65*, 125, 129. *See also* fairs; libraries; Presbyterian Church

Dumond, Isaac and John, 27, 28, 33, 60, 61

Earsley, Maria, 33, 55

Eddy, Otis, cotton mill of, 112, 116, 187, 188

education, 111–32

Egbert, W. Grant, 120, *121*, 123

Eight-Square Schoolhouse, 15, 64, *65*, 129

electric lights, 44–45

Ellis Hollow, 67, 172, 175

Ellis, John and Peleg, 66–67

Elm Tree Inn, *72*, 72

Enfield Creek, 22, 68; mills on, 69, 164–65

Enfield Glen. *See* Robert H. Treman State Park

Enfield, town of, 34, *69*; creation, 15, 40, 69, 83; schools in, 68, *130*; settlement, 33, 68. *See also* Robert H. Treman State Park

Erie Canal, 15, 42, 52; role in trade and transportation, 93–95, 104, 168, 191

factories, 54, 56, 71, 81, 94; in Ithaca, 112, 116, 187–90, 203–5, *205*. *See also* mills

fairs: annual, 67, 172; for county exhibitions, 171–72; Dryden, 65–66, *66*, 172; Ithaca Fairground, *40*, *171*, 172

Fall Creek, 22, 50, 64, 71, 206; bridges over, 25, 54, *72*, 93, 105, *157*; dam across, 93, 112, 173; mills, 41, 54, *54*, 112, 188–89, *189*

farming, farms. *See* agriculture

financial crisis: in 1837, 15, 32, 42, 97, 190; in 1873, 16, 42, 100; Great Depression, 18, 138

Finger Lakes: early exploration of, 24; geological development, 21–22; and tourism, 164, 194

Finger Lakes Library System, 134

[223]

Index

Finger Lakes Park Commission, 69–70, 164
fire(s): companies, 41, 137; in Ithaca, 16, 43, 188, 189, 196, 197, 200, 217; in Newfield, 17, 80; in Trumansburg, 86
Fiske, Jennie McGraw, 50, 133, 136, 217n5. *See also* McGraw, Jennie
Five Mile Creek. *See* Enfield Creek
flood(s), 39–40, *40*, *84*, 165; control, 52–53, 163; destruction by, 17, 18, 77–78, 81, 83–84
Florence. *See* Newfield
Forest Home (Free Hollow), *54*, 54–55, 188, 189
Freeville, 17, 38, 64, *66*, 66, 100
Fugitive Slave Law, 15, 152, 154

Gannett, Frank, 171, 201
George Junior Republic, 17, 66, 128–29
George, William R., 128
Gere, Luther, 43, 194; tavern of, 194–95, 196
Gerhart, Tom and Penny, 193
Goodwin's Point, 32, 82
gorges, 22, *23*, 50, 68, 82, *92*, *157*, *166*, *167*, *206*; beauty of, 11, *156*, 164. *See also* bridges; parks; waterfalls
government: county, 37, 39, 139, 209; early community, 33–34, 41, 59; Ithaca city, 51–52
Grange, 16, 61, 175; League Federation, 192–93
Grant's Coffee House, 195
Grant, Thomas, 25
Griswold, Abram and Edward, 64–65, 158
Groton: Bridge Manufacturing Company, 17, 71, *92*, *174*, 202; Carriage Company, 17, *71*, *71*, 202
Groton, town of: formation, 15; incorporated village in, 38, 71; manufacturing in, 38, 70, *71*, *71*, *92*, *174*, 201–3, *203*; settlement of, 33, 70; small communities in, 71–73

Halseyville, 84–85, *85*
Hanner, Jabez, 33, 68
Hector, 16, 25, 34, 36, 37

Hicks, Benjamin, 33, 70
Hinepaugh, Peter, 27, 28
historical societies, 16, 39, 53, 135, 184; DeWitt Historical Society, 53, 184, 198, 214; Historic Ithaca, 18, 53, 184, 198, 214; regional history collection, 214
hotels: bed and breakfast, 199; in Ithaca, 32, 42, 43, 195–98; resort, 85–86, *142*, 169–70, 199; watering spas, 58, *59*, 199. *See also* Clinton House; Dryden Springs House; Elm Tree Inn; Ithaca Hotel; Tompkins House
Horton, Henry B., 204
Husa, Karel, 180

Indians, 14, 33; as early settlers, 22, 24–25, 27, 74, 78, 82, 193; Sullivan's campaign against, 11, 14, 24–25, 74, 89; surrender of land by, 25, 29, 78
industries, 186–87, 190–91, 203–4; adding machines, 208; boat building, 73, 77, 95, 190; bridge building, 17, 70, 71, *92*, *174*, 202; carriages, 17, *71*, *71*, 202; cement, 73, 78; cotton manufacture, 112, 116, 187, 188; distillation of alcohol, 58, 74, 137, 188, 191; flouring mills, 15, 81, 187, 188; gun making, 54–55, 188, 203, 208; higher education, 111, 201; high-technology, 208, 211–12; lumbering, 64, 81, 187; movie making, 161, *178*, 186, 205–7, *206*; paper, 188–89; tourism, 84, 85–86, 156, 164, 194–99; typewriters, 70, 71, 202–3, *203*, 208. *See also* agriculture; mills; salt
Inlet: flood control channel, 52–53, 163; Creek, 22, 33, 61, 78, 93, 95, 98; settlement along, 138, *139*, 163; Valley, 24, 97
Iroquois Confederacy: formation, 22; role in Revolutionary War, 24; territory, 25, 29
Ithaca: establishment of, 27–32; early views of, 24, 25, 32, 149, 190, 218n18, 218n21; map of, *30*, *31*; role in county, 38–39; train service,

[224]

96–103. *See also* church(es); commercial buildings; fairs; hotels; mills; residences; taverns
Ithaca, city of: businesses in, 203–9; charter for, 51–52; establishment of, 17, 51; extension of, 105; streets, *88, 108, 136, 168*; urban development and renewal, 53–54, 135, 214; water supply, 143–44, 165
Ithaca, town of: communities in, 54–55; creation of, 40–41, 195
Ithaca, village of: commercial schemes for, 42, 96, 186, 190–91; as county seat, 37, 38; in 1860s, 43, *47*; in 1880s, 43–50, *48–49*; incorporation, 15, 41, 195; streets, 43, *51*; as transportation center, 34, 41–42, 95–96; water supply, 43–44
Ithaca College, *44*, 125, 128, 178, 179; campuses, 123, *124*, 143, 158; establishment of, 18, 122; role, 123. *See also* Ithaca Conservatory of Music
Ithaca Commons, 19, 53–54, 106, 182, 211, 212
Ithaca companies: Calendar Clock, 16, 204–5, *205*; Ithaca Gun, 17, 188, 203, 208–9; Sign Works, 204
Ithaca Conservatory of Music: buildings, *44, 46,* 120–21, *122,* 158, 177; founding and development, 17, 120–22; schools of, 121–22, 181. *See also* Ithaca College
Ithaca Falls, *157,* 209
Ithaca Hotel, 195; first, 14, 16, 43, *45,* 91, 190; second, 43, 53, 196, *197*
Ithaca Journal, The, 199–201; first issue, 15, 43, 199
Ithaca Opera Association, 179, 180
Ithaca Street Railway, 17, 51, *87;* impact of, 105–6; and Renwick Park development, 160–61; service, 104–5; and the Short Line, 101, 106; trolley loop, 93, *105,* 105

Jacksonville, 83, 141, 155, 193
Johnson, George A., 154
Joy, Benjamin, 137, 155

LaBarr, Eugene, 77
Lake Ridge, 74, 78, 102

Lansing, town of, 38, 159; formation, 15, 74; incorporated village in, 19, 38, 78, 175; industries, 73, 78, 95, 194, *195;* and railroads, 76–77; as retail center, 73, 78, 212; settlement of, 32, 73–74; small communities in, 74
Lehigh Valley Railroad: Black Diamond, 18, 102, 103; consolidation by, 17, 57, 77, 100; service, 102, *103;* station, 103, 104, *148*
Libertyville (South Lansing), 15, 74, 76, 76, 199
libraries, 65, 132–37; early, 32, 42, 83–84, 132, 133, 135; Southworth (Dryden), 65, *133,* 133; Tompkins County Public, 19, 134–35, 204; Ulysses Philomathic (Trumansburg), 83–84, 132–33. *See also* Cornell Public Library
Lincoln, Abraham, 16, 76, 133
Livingston Purchase, 78
Locke (Military Township), 15, 25, 33, 36, 70, 74
Ludlow, Silas, Henry, and Thomas, 32, 74
Ludlowville, 25, 34, 74, 75, 77, 100, 107, 150, 194

McDowell, Robert, 27
McGraw-Fiske mansion, *48–49, 50,* 50, 217n5
McGraw, Jane, 50, 136, 147
McGraw, Jennie, 65, 115, *116,* 120. *See also* Fiske, Jennie McGraw
McGraw, John, 31, 50, 65, 136, 147
McGraw, Joseph, 65, 133
McIntyre, Arnold, 54
McIntyre, J. V., 76, 171
McLallen, James, 82, 85
McLean, 70, 71–72, *72,* 107, 192
markets, public, 41, 192; Ithaca Farmers', 158, 193, 214
Markle, Abram, house of, *29,* 29, 194
medicine and health: early doctors, 140–41; hospitals, 18, 19, 39, 142–43, 144; patent medicines, 137, 141; public health, 15, 18, 143–45; sanatoriums, 64, 141–42, 143
Melotte, George W., 145

[225]

Index

mercantile trade: early stores, 45, 56, 61, 68, 82, 190; modern shopping areas, 53–54, 73, 212; Rothschild's, 46, 120, *136*, *168*, 212
Military Tract, 26, 27–28, 38, 78; townships in, 25, 32, 36, 63, 73
Miller, William Henry, 47, 50, 133, 136, 152, 185
Milliken Station (NYSE&G), 77, 78, 102
mills: early, 27, 33, 187; Caroline, 56, 59; Danby, 61; Dryden, 64, 187; Enfield, 69, 165; Ithaca, 32, 41, 47, 54, *83*, 187–90, *189*; Lansing, 74; Newfield, 79, 81. *See also* factories; industries
Milton (Military Township), 15, 25, 32, 36, 74
Minier, Daniel D., 76
Morrill Land Grant Act, 16, 115
Morse Borg-Warner, 207
Morse Chain Company, 17, 86, 193; diversification of, 207–8
Morse, Frank, 86, 207, 208
Morse, Samuel F. B., 42, 108, 112
Mott's Corners, 56
Mott, William, II, 56
Mulks, Benoni, 56
museums, 184–85, 198
musical groups, 175–76, *176*, 179–80, *183*; church choirs, 183–84; collegiate, 175, 177, 181–83. *See also* bands
Myers, 78, 107, 159, *195*
Myers, Andrew, 32, 74

National Cash Register (NCR), 208
New Deal programs, 18, 138, 161, 165
Newfield Covered Bridge, 15, 79, *80*, 80, 93, *94*
Newfield, town of, 17, 25, 79, *80*, 98, 107; boundaries, 15, 37, 38, 80; incorporation as village, 17, 38, 80; industries, 15, 81, 193; settlement of, 33, 78–79; schools in, 81, 128, 131; small communities in, 79
Newman, Jared T., 161, 162
newspapers, 15, 41, 43, 52, 171, 193, 199–201
New York State: Agricultural College, 115; Board of Regents, 125, 127, 132; colleges at Cornell, 118, 119; SUNY, 119, 123–24, 127
Nina (East Newfield), 79, 98
Nivison, Samantha, 16, 117, 141–42
North, Thomas, cabin of, 74

Old Bush Stand, 58, 59, 194
Old City Hall (Village Hall), 15, 42, 47, *215*; demolition, 53, 214; statue in front of, *136*, 138

parks: forests, 160, 164; marinas, 19, 78, 159, 163, 164, 167; municipal, 18, 41, 51, 53, 77–78, 156–64; state, 18, 164–67
Peer, Sherman, 134
Perrin, John, 33, 70
Peruville, 71
pioneers: daily life, 34–36; as farmers, 34, 187, 192; first settlements, 27–34; travel for, 28, 32, 89. *See also* settlers
Poney Hollow, 25, 33, 78
population, 39, 87, 213–14
postal service: air mail, 107, *109*; early, 64, 70, 79, 91, 107; postmasters, 14, 58, 61, 79, 107; rural free delivery, 17, 107, *108*
post offices: in communities today, 61, 72, 107; early, 64, 70, 82, 107; Ithaca, 107, *108*, *215*; Speedsville, 56, 58–59, 107
Presbyterian Church: Dryden, 65, 150, 159; Ithaca, 41, 43, *131*, 134, 150–51, 158, *159*; Ulysses, 83, 133, 149–50
professions: banking, 210–11; dental, 145–46; legal, 209–10; medical, 15, 140–42. *See also* banks; medicine and health

Quigg, David, 190

racetracks, 48–49, 66, 77, 160, 172
railroad(s), 67, *99*; building boom, 42, 98, 100; charters, 15, 42, 96; early schemes, 95–96; routes, 97–98, *99*, 100, 102; service today, 77, 102–3; for transport of goods, 42, 77, 102–3, 194. *See also* travel
railroad companies, 110; Cayuga Lake, 16, 77, 100, 105, 161, 169; Delaware,

[226]

Index

Lackawanna & Western (DL&W), 98, 100, 102; Geneva, Ithaca & Sayre, 61, 85, 100; Ithaca & Athens, 98, 100; Ithaca & Cortland, 98; Ithaca & Owego (I&O), 15, 16, 31–32, 94–97; New York, Auburn & Lansing, 77, 101–2; Short Line, 17, 77, 101, 106; Utica, Ithaca & Elmira, 16, 57, 64, 71–72, 100, *101*. *See also* Lehigh Valley Railroad

recreation and pastimes: early, 156–57, 167; parades, *51, 168*, 168; sports, 172–73; tourism, 84, 85–86, 156, 168–71, 194–99. *See also* fairs; musical groups; parks; theatrical groups

religious organizations. *See* church(es); church organizations

Renwick Heights, 54, 160

Renwick Park, 18, *106*, 160, 179, 180, 206; development, 105, 161; pier at, *162, 169*, 170

Renwick, James Jeffrey, 161

Renwick, Robert Jeffrey, 160

Renwick Tract, 54, 95, 105, 160–61

residences, 56, 67; as hospitals, 142–43, 144, *145*; as hotels, 85, 199; in Ithaca, 29, 29, 43, 46, 47, 50, 65, *136, 185*, 185, 194; in Trumansburg, 15, *83*, 83, 85. *See also* Boardman House; McGraw-Fiske mansion

Revolutionary War, 24; veterans, land for, 25, 27, 64, 79, 82

Rich, David, 33, 55

roads: Bridle Road, 34, 89; early, 14, 34, 82, 88–89; modern highways, 87, 89, 91; toll, 34, 39, 90; wooden plank, 91. *See also* turnpikes

Robert H. Treman State Park, 18, *23*, 69–70, *70, 164,* 164; old mill at, *68*, 69, 164–65

Robertson, George, 33, 64, 67

Robinson, C. S., airline of, 18, 104, *109*

Rogues Harbor Inn, 15, 76, 195; description, 76, 199; names for, 76, 77, 199; train link to, 101–2, 171

Rulloff, Edward, 77

Sage, Henry W., 118, 143
Sage, William H., 92–93

Salmon Creek, 22, 74, *75*, 77–78; viaduct over, 91

salt: companies, 77, 78, 102–3, 160, 194, *195*; as county industry, 73, 78, 187, 193–94; as important commodity, 22, 25; trade in, 32, 191; transport of, 42, 77, 102–3, 194

school buildings, 53, *126*, 130, 132; changes in, 53, 175; early schoolhouses, 15, 33, 58, 64, *65*, 81, 129–30, *130*; Ithaca High, 47, 52, 53, 88, *126*, 130, *131*; in Trumansburg, *127*, 132

schools, private, 125, 128; Cascadilla School, 126–27; Immaculate Conception, 127–28; Ithaca Academy, 82, 125, *126*, 129, 131, 135; Trumansburg Academy, 82, 125, *127*, 132

schools, public, 81, 125–26, 132; districts, 131–32; early, 41, 58; system in NY, 15, 16, 129, 130, 131

Schurman, Jacob Gould, 119

Seabring, Richard, 79

settlers: early white, 14; Indian, 22, 24, 74, 78; origin of, 27, 32, 33, 34, 55, 56, 57, 74, 79, 81

Silent City, 17, 138, *139*, 163

Six Mile Creek, 22, 43, 97–98; bridge over, 57, 57, 100, *101*; Ithaca water supply from, 43–44, 143–44, 165

Slater, Levi and Thomas, 58

Slaterville, 56, 57–58, *90*, 199; also named Slaterville Springs, 58, *59*, 107

slavery: abolition in NY, 15, 56; proclamation ending, 16. *See also* black(s); slaves

slaves, 14, 56, 58, 60, 152, 154–55

Smith Corona Marchant (SCM), 71, 123; formation, 18, 202–3

Smith, Goldwin, 116, 118, 218n11

Sodus Bay, *26*; proposed canal, 94, 95

South Lansing, 74, 199; depot at, 77, 101, 171

Southwick, Solomon, 190, 218n19, 218n21

Speed, John Jacob, 56, 58–59, 60
Speed, John Jacob, Jr., 58
Speed, Joseph, 55–56, 60, 140

[227]

Index

Speedsville, 56, 58–59, 107; covered bridge at, 59, *60*
Speed tavern, 56, 90
Sprague, Joseph B., 44
stagecoach, *45*, *195*; as public transportation, 90, 95, 104; routes, 34, 41–42, 91
steamboats, 42, *169*, 169–70, *170*; *DeWitt Clinton*, 42, 95, 169; *Enterprise*, 15, 95, 190; *Frontenac*, 16, 17, 86, *169*, *170*, 170; landing sites, *48–49*, 86, 94, 95, 100, *106*, *162*, *169*, 169, *170*, 170
Stephens, Henry Morse, 118, 175
Stewart Avenue, 105; bridges, 52, *92*, 92, 93, *157*, 202, 206
Stewart, David B., 51–52, 92, 161
Stewart, Edwin C., 161
Stewart Park, 51, 101, 160; concerts at, 181, 182; development, 18, 53, 161–62
Sullivan, John, campaign against the Indians, 11, 14, 24–25, 74, 89
Susquehanna River, 24, 56, 154; as pioneer route, 27, 32, 74; and transportation network, 94, 96
Sweet, Amos, 33, 64

Taughannock Creek, 22; bridge across, 84–85, *85*
Taughannock Falls, 82, 84, *167*; hotels at, 85–86, 199; State Park, 18, 86, 165
Taughannock Point. *See* Goodwin's Point
taverns, 82; in Caroline, 56, 58, *90*, 194; in Ithaca, 32, 82, 107, 194–95, *196*, 198; on turnpikes, 68, 90, 104
telegraph, 15, 87, 107–8, 109; Ezra Cornell's work in, 42, 108, 112
telephone(s), 87; companies, 110; first, 44, 108; service, 17, 109–10
temperance movement, 56; in Ithaca, *136*, 137–38, 147; in Lansing, 74, 76, 77, 137; in Trumansburg, 84, 137
terrain: beauty of, 11, 22, 156, 164; problems created by, 39, 87–88, 96, 110, 186
theaters: college, 179–80; in Ithaca, 17, 163–64, 177–81, *178*; opera houses, 86, 177, 180, *183*
theatrical groups, 175–76, 179–80
Thomas, James, 33, 78
Thomas-Morse Aviation Company, 163, 208
Tompkins Cortland Community College (TC3), 19, 66, 123, 124–25
Tompkins County: big business in, 207–9; commercial development, 186–87, 213; early scene, 21–22, 24; as educational center, 111, 156; geological development, 21–22; isolation of, 87–88, 110, 191; organization of, 15, 25–26, 36–37, 38; resources, 22, 25, 187; scenic beauty, 11, 22, 156; social services, 39, 137, 138–40; as special environment, 12, 40, 88, 214, 215; towns and villages in, 38
Tompkins County Courthouse: first 36, 37; Old, 15, 36, 209, *210*; present, 18, 209–10
Tompkins County, organizations in: Area Development Corporation, 211–12; Arts Council, 156, 176; Chamber of Commerce, 212; Dental Society, 145–46; Medical Society, 15, 140, 141
Tompkins, Daniel D., *35*, 37, 196
Tompkins House, *51*, 91, 195, 196
Townley, Richard and Charles, 74
transportation, 87; air, 103; bus services, 104, 106–7, 117; early, 34, 42, 87, 88–89; importance of, 39, 87; network, plans for, 93–96; public, 51, 90, 95, 104–7. *See also* Ithaca Street Railway; railroads; travel
travel: early, 34, 89, 91; excursions on the lake, 42, 95, 100, 161, 168–70; railroad excursions, 100, 101–2, *103*, 169, 171
Treman, Abner, 32, 82
Treman, Allan H., 164; marina named for, 19, 163, 164, 167
Treman, Jared, 69, 165
Treman, Robert H., *176*; gifts of land for parks, 69, 164, 165; lake named for, 165; park named for, 69, 70, 164

[228]

Index

Triphammer Bridge, 93, 105; name for, 55
Trumansburg, 18, *83*, *84*, 85; businesses in, 85–86, 207; incorporated village of, 16, 38, 86; names for, 82, 137; Opera Block, 85, *86*, 86, 180; schools in, 82, 125–26, *127*, 131–32; settlement of, 32, 82, 83. *See also* libraries; Presbyterian Church
Trumansburg Creek, 81, 83–84
Tubman, Harriet, 154
turnpikes: description, 89–91; Ithaca & Geneva, 14, 85, 91; Ithaca & Owego, 14, 61, 91; as toll roads, 34, 39, 90. *See also* Catskill Turnpike
typhoid fever epidemic, 17, 143–44

Ulysses, town of, 14, 15, 38, 81, 138; creation of, 36, 40, 83; settlements in, 82–83. *See also* Trumansburg
Underground Railroad, 15, 61, 152, 154
Van Rensselaer, Martha, 118, *119*
Village Hall (Ithaca). *See* Old City Hall

Wait, Lucien, 126
War of 1812, 15, 37, 58, 67, 89
Washington, George, 14, 24

waterfalls, 22, *23*, 24–25, 75, 82, 84, 165, *167*
Webb, Peter, 60
West Danby, 61, 98, 107, 175
Weyburn, Samuel, 32, 82
Wharton Studios, 161, 178, 205–6, *206*
White, Andrew Dickson, 113, *114*, 116, 119, 168; plans for Cornell University, 114–15, 117; recruitment of faculty by, 118, 175
White, Daniel, 66
Willard State Hospital, 115, 139
Williams, Josiah B., 97, 142–43
Willow Glen, 33, 64
Wisner, William, 43, 150–51
Women's Christian Temperance Union, 138, 147; drinking fountain put up by, *136*, 138
Women's Community Building, 18, 127, 147–49
Woodworth, Jonathan, 27
Wyckoff, Edward G., 93, 105
Wyckoff, William O., 109, 110, 128

Yaple, Jacob and John, 27, 28, 33, 60–61, 187
YMCA, 15, 16, 174–75, 200, *215*; new building of, 73, 175

[229]